Come Holy Spirit

Peter De Rosa was born in north London in 1932 and educated at the Jesuit College of St Ignatius. He read Philosophy and Theology at St Edmund's College and, having graduated from the Gregorian University in Rome, he lectured for five years at St Edmund's. He was Vice-Principal of Corpus Christi, London, an international institute for religious education, for five years, and is currently a radio producer.

Come Holy Spirit

The Life of God in the
Life of Men

PETER DE ROSA

Collins
FONTANA BOOKS

First published in Fontana Books 1975
Second Impression September 1975

© Peter De Rosa 1975

Made and printed in Great Britain by
William Collins Sons & Co Ltd Glasgow

FOR M.E.

He will grow old and you will grow old,
He will love you and you love him.
May your sun set in a blaze of gold
    And the night creep in.

Contents

Contents

Introduction

Already the story is becoming legendary. A prospective Japanese convert from Shintoism to Christianity remarks to the painstaking missionary: 'Most High Person of Honourable Father, him I understand. Honourable Son, him also I understand. But, please, be so favourable as to tell me, who is that Honourable Bird?'

This is not the first time that the Spirit's descent 'like a dove' (Mark 1:10) upon Jesus at his baptism has caused perplexity.

Gustave Flaubert's famous tale *A Simple Heart*[1] has as its heroine a faithful serving woman named Felicity. Thwarted in love and not robust in health, Felicity found solace in religion. The rural things around her made the gospel stories come alive. She loved lambs because Christ was the Lamb of God; she loved doves because of the Holy Spirit.

Her problem was how to imagine the Spirit. He was not only a bird, she knew, but a flame and a breath of air as well.

One day a parrot from America called Loulou was delivered to her mistress's house. Loulou had a fine green body, a blue forehead and a golden throat but, because of his tiresome habits, he was handed over to the sole custody of Felicity. They often talked together and, as they talked, the lonely Felicity grew to love him.

It was a winter's day of tragic dimensions when Loulou was found dead on the floor of his cage.

On her mistress's advice, the heart-broken Felicity sent Loulou to a taxidermist to be stuffed. Afterwards, how life-like he looked sitting upright on a branch that had been screwed to a mahogany base. From that time onwards, Loulou took his honoured place among the other religious bric-à-brac in Felicity's room.

In church, Felicity used to sit for hours gazing at the stained-glass window depicting the Holy Spirit. Through the association in her mind, the parrot became sanctified. God the Father, she thought, must surely have chosen not a dove but a parrot who could talk to make his purposes known. At night she even prayed to the Holy Spirit in front of her feathered friend.

At length, when Felicity was dying, as the sweet-smelling smoke of incense clouded her room, 'she thought she saw in the opening heavens a gigantic parrot, hovering above her head.'

In *A Simple Heart*, Flaubert was not writing a polemic against Christianity. The picture of Felicity is too tenderly drawn for that. She was one of that devout multitude who, in Flaubert's words, 'did not understand or try to understand' Church dogmas. She loved simpler things: the harmony of bells, the evening light on the edge of the marshes, the cool walls and the stillness of a church in summer, a stained-glass window depicting the Holy Spirit as a dove. Her one mistake – and who would say she did not benefit from it? – was to take a biblical image over-literally. Even Luke the evangelist does not hesitate to develop Mark's plain words 'like a dove'. He writes that after Jesus was baptized 'the Holy Spirit descended upon him *in bodily form*, as a dove' (Luke 3:22).

There are two extremes to be avoided here. The first is to allow the *language* of dogmas fashioned centuries ago to tyrannize over us and to construct mere puzzles for the mind. Orthodox formulas then become the bearers of highly unorthodox meanings. The second extreme is to misread biblical imagery and symbolism as Felicity did and, in consequence, to take literally what is meant to be a poetic insight into the things of God, a flare thrown into the dark night of infinite reality. Of the two extremes perhaps the former does more harm since it does not in any sense lift up the human spirit. It is not close enough to prayer.

THE MISSION OF THE DOVE

Any child knows that the dove is first mentioned in the Bible in the story of Noah and the Flood (Gen. 8). It is only when the waters subside that the dove appears. It represents God's kindness and his forgiveness of a world whose sins had brought it to so great a calamity. The Hebrew word for dove is *jonah*. The Old Testament book that tells the parable of a reluctant prophet being swallowed by a big fish after refusing to preach repentance to the hated Ninevites is really, therefore, *The Book of the Dove*. Jonah, despite his loathing for the task, eventually identifies himself with the saving work God gave him to do; and the Ninevites, who do not know their right hand from their left, repent in sackcloth and ashes. Once more a dove has been the messenger of God's kindness and mercy.

Scholars generally agree that this splendid parable was written in the fourth century BC. It was a period when Israel, far too intent on her own survival, had ceased to care about the nations surrounding her. Jonah evidently stands for Israel herself whom God is enticing out of her exclusivism to become the chosen messenger of his pardon and peace. It is worth noting that the Psalmist actually refers to Israel as a dove: 'Do not deliver the soul of thy dove to the wild beasts' (Ps. 74:19).

This is the background against which we should read the story of Jesus' baptism. The Holy Spirit came down upon Jesus like a dove, like a Jonah. From that time on, Jesus becomes 'the Missioner of God', the one who is charged to spread abroad the message of God's forgiveness freely bestowed by God on all the world. The only sign that Jesus claimed to give unbelievers was 'the sign of Jonah', that is, the message that God forgives everyone who repents.

Current references to 'Hawks and Doves' suggest that the dove has been reinstated in the West as a symbol of peace, of the ending of isolation. But perhaps only the poet can satisfactorily interpret for us the imagery of the Holy Spirit descending like a dove. In his poem *God's Grandeur*, Gerard Manley Hopkins, after acknowledging that every generation has by sinning smudged and smeared God's glory in the world, goes on to say:

And for all this, nature is never spent;
   There lives the dearest freshness deep down things;
And though the last lights off the black West went
   Oh, morning, at the brown brink eastward, springs –
Because the Holy Ghost over the bent
   World broods with warm breast and with ah! bright
     wings.[2]

'The Holy Ghost' is the subject of this book. From several alternatives I have chosen to explore the many images by means of which the Spirit's action is expressed in scripture. These images, I believe, speak to us of the mystery of God in the simplest and profoundest possible way. It is strange that stories, myths, images, symbols, parables, are still considered by many Christians to be too inaccurate, too unsophisticated, to teach us about God, seeing that from start to finish, the Bible is a picture-book of God. Surely no one would suggest that there is anything in subsequent theology to compare with the brilliant images used by the author of the fourth gospel? Too much theology merits the comment of the poet Edwin Muir: 'The Word made flesh is here made word again.'

THE CATHOLICISM OF THE SPIRIT

When belief becomes dis-incarnate, the impression is given that religion is the preserve of religious people, especially of those people who grasp or at least are familiar with the formulas of religion. In fact, Christ's Spirit, being God's Spirit, has always been among men, blowing where he wills. In the First Letter of Peter we read: 'The prophets who prophesied of the grace that was to be yours searched and inquired about this salvation; they inquired what person or time was indicated *by the Spirit of Christ within them* when predicting the sufferings of Christ and the subsequent glory' (1:10-11). It is equally true that the Spirit of Christ is at work wherever men and women carry on Christ's reconciling mission, even unknown to themselves. 'Lord, when did we see thee hungry and feed thee?' the righteous will ask. And Christ's answer: 'As you did it to one of the least of these my brethren, you did it to me' (Matt. 25:37, 40). The anonymous Christ who has something to give feeds and cares for the anonymous Christ who has nothing. Even beneath this splendid dual anonymity, Christ's Spirit is re-fashioning the hearts of men. The Good Samaritan did not know he was binding up the wounds of Christ. He probably did not even suspect that he was good.

This is a reminder that Christ's Spirit is no more the unique possession of Christians than is Christ or God himself. The Spirit of Christ is a power that all men can feel, the life-force that floods the universe. His is the impulse that causes rivers to run, seas to ebb and flow, hearts to go on beating, love to conquer everything.

I like very much the ending Georges Bernanos gave to *The Diary of a Country Priest*. The tormented, tubercular curé is dying. He who ministered so lovingly to his flock has now no one to offer him the consolations of the Church. The friend by his bedside expresses regret that he should have to pass away like this. But the curé whispers in his ear: 'Does it matter? Grace is . . . everywhere.'³ Just then, he died.

Grace is everywhere and for everyone. For grace is the presence of God. God cannot charge for anything, least of all for himself. Hence, grace is free as air; it drops like rain on good and bad alike. Unfortunately, we, like Jonah, find it hard to reconcile ourselves to the catholicism of God.

It was the supposed lack of genuine catholicism in the Church that led the brilliant young French woman, Simone Weil, to refuse baptism. She preferred, as she put it, to remain where she had always been, 'at the intersection of Christianity and everything that is not Christianity.'⁴ She wanted to stay outside the city among all the lovely things which had led her to the city-gate but to which, she believed, the Church refused entrance. Simone Weil's motive was right. The Church is not something to which we can be attached as to an earthly city. Only the kingdom of God which consists of meekness, generosity, humility, poverty, can command absolute obedience. In the kingdom there are many Samaritans who simply found themselves there by facing squarely and lovingly the challenges of their life.

Of course, Christ has given a new and distinctive shape to his disciples' experience of life. They 'organize' reality as he taught them. They have learned through him how to interpret suffering, riches, joy, disaster, death. That is why they call him 'Lord' and join with him in addressing God as 'Father'.

Nevertheless, most human beings – some dimly, some

vividly – perceive that 'There lives the dearest freshness deep down things'. Life is unfathomable, mysterious; and before it they can only bow in humility. They sense they are constantly drawing on a Power in which they are suffused, a Power that is in them but not of them, a Power to which their hearts cry out in crises and excessive joy. And if there is no faith, there is what Browning calls *The Grand Perhaps*:

> How can we guard our unbelief,
> Make it bear fruit to us? – the problem here.
> Just when we are safest, there's a sunset-touch,
> A fancy from a flower-bell, some one's death,
> A chorus-ending from Euripides, –
> And that's enough for fifty hopes and fears
> As old and new at once as nature's self,
> To rap and knock and enter in our soul.[5]

I think it was Rossetti who said that the most agonizing time for the atheist is when he feels happy and grateful – and has no one to thank.

Artists in their quest for beauty, scientists in their relentless pursuit of understanding, and particularly lovers who know that every value pales in comparison with love – all sense in their own way the life that is beyond life. Who can say how many people come to a vivid appreciation of this when they are about to die? For this *hollowing* can also be a *hallowing*. The self-emptying of the dying is not merely the occasion of great humility; perhaps most discover too the great brotherliness of death. It shows in the very features of the dying; a strange, hitherto unnoticed family resemblance. What, after all, did all life's differences mean in face of the frightening and yet elevating democracy of death?

And what of death itself? It is a life-giving reality since, as Herbert Samuel said, unless there were death, there could be no new life either. We can imagine a world without

new birth; we can imagine another without death. What
we cannot imagine is a world with birth but without death.
The earth could not sustain such a multitude. The dying
must grasp however darkly that their death makes possible
new births, new hopes, new desires upon the earth. Finally,
death brings everyone into fellowship with the Crucified
who 'emptied himself' (Phil. 2:7). Since Christ died, there
is no way now of avoiding him or of escaping a decision for
him or against him. Experience seems to show that a great
number of people die humbly, forgivingly, hopefully – like
Christ.

In these and countless other ways, the Christ of God has
always been in the world and always will be. Often dumb
and nameless, he found in Jesus of Nazareth a perfect voice
and a perfect name. That is why Jesus is Emmanuel, God-
with-us. His story is the story of Adam, of Everyman; the
Christian festivals that commemorate his life, death and
resurrection celebrate the birth and renewal of mankind.

The biblical images I have chosen to develop in this book
are rich and overlapping as all authentic poetic images
must be. Their richness points to the as yet untapped
possibilities of life in the universe. They teach us that life is
stronger than death; that all men inhabit a single spiritual
universe in which Christ's Spirit is the source of life,
warmth, energy, light.

Before examining the biblical images, we need to clarify
the language we use of what is generally called 'the mystery
of the Trinity'. Christianity should be pointing to the path
all men must take if they are to reach their destined fulness
of life: the path that leads to God through Christ in the
power of the Spirit. Instead, abstruse doctrines often seem
to erect a high fence around an enclosure in which only
Christians may walk. The way Christ meant us to organize
the whole of human experience has become for many a mere
matter of recondite formulas to which nobody but Christians

have access. I think this idea is profoundly mistaken and it is worth trying to put it right. In common with a character in *A Passage to India* by E. M. Forster, 'I like mysteries but I rather dislike muddles.'

1. *God, Christ and the Spirit*

I suspect that the medieval theologian Peter Abelard is better known for his love-affair with Héloise than for his distinguished contribution to theology. However, in Helen Waddell's famous book *Peter Abelard*, his theology also comes under scrutiny. The massive, friendly Gilles de Vannes, Canon of Notre Dame, is in conversation with one of Abelard's fiery young disciples, Pierre, about the master's latest treatise on the Trinity. Pierre asks:

> 'Have you read the *De Trinitate*, Gilles?'
> Gilles nodded. 'It is more than his accusers have, I'll be bound.'
> 'And is it heretical?'
> 'Of course it is heretical. Every book that ever was written about the Trinity is heretical, barring the Athanasian Creed. And even that only saves itself by contradicting everything it says as fast as it says it.'[6]

This reply gives a fair impression of the average reader's response to that particular creed: 'Eternal Father, eternal Son, eternal Holy Spirit; and yet not three Eternals but one Eternal . . . One Father, not three Fathers; one Son, not three Sons; one Holy Spirit, not three Holy Spirits. And in this Trinity there is no before or after, no more or less, but all three co-eternal persons are equal with each other so that in everything we must venerate unity in Trinity and Trinity in unity. Whoever wants to be saved must think this of the Trinity.'

The reader may be pardoned for thinking instead that it must be somewhat difficult to be saved! The creed calls to mind one of Leo Rosten's stories in *The Joys of Yiddish*. An elderly Jew was knocked down in front of a church. As he lay there half-conscious, a priest hurried out and prepared to administer the last rites. 'Do you believe in God the Father, God the Son and God the Holy Ghost?' At which the old Jew gasped: 'I'm dying and he asks me riddles?'

Even the clever, controversial Bishop Pike used to say that the age-old doctrine of the Trinity should be abandoned since it is a stumbling block to the spread of Christianity. Apart from anything else, it leads to the accusation of polytheism. As he once quipped: 'The Muslims offer one God and three wives; we offer three Gods and one wife. No wonder Christianity is losing in Africa.'

There can be no doubt that most Christians are puzzled by what is called 'the mystery of the Trinity or three persons in one God'. In my view, much of their mystification has little or nothing to do with the mystery itself but stems rather from an obscure use of language. They are at a loss to know what the words 'nature' and 'person' mean and how anything, God included, can be one and three at the same time.

The phrase 'one nature' seems to indicate a divine common denominator of Father, Son and Holy Spirit; but if they have *divinity* in common, how can they possibly be different? Three men can have humanity in common and be different in colour, height, shape, and so on. But what is there in God that could be other than divine? Then, 'person' in current usage means a distinct individual *with a mind and will of his own*. Theologians are quick to warn us that this cannot be part of an orthodox definition of the persons of the Trinity. If each divine person had a mind and will of his own, there would be three beings or three Gods.

This alone shows that language has changed its meaning considerably since 'person' was first applied to Father, Son and Spirit in the Latin Church. The naming of the Spirit as 'the Holy Ghost' has added to the confusion by making the Spirit appear to be some kind of spook or spectral shape.

Is there any other approach which the ordinary Christian can adopt to help him grasp these matters in a fruitful way? The answer is obvious. There is a book which speaks about God without recourse to abstract, metaphysical ideas like nature, person, Trinity; and without 'contradicting' everything it says as soon as it says it. The Bible is that book. It is completely free from the fine distinctions and what can only be called the *anxiety* of so many text-books on the Trinity. However, it would be unjust to disparage the efforts of speculative theologians. In the pre-scientific era, theology was almost the only exciting and disciplined study men could engage in. Further, it could be plausibly argued that the Church has had to go through anxious times when the faith was preserved by those so-called fine distinctions. No one could possibly read Augustine, Abelard and Aquinas without the deepest respect and admiration for their piety and learning.

But it remains true that our age, though certainly sophisticated, is in a curious way far more in tune with biblical times than with the vanished worlds of the Athanasian Creed and medieval theology. The reason is, I believe, that the Bible speaks in concrete, poetical terms and uses the eternal language of elemental things – wind, water, fire, the breath we inhale and exhale to sustain our fragile bodies. Perhaps, too, the biblical images speak so powerfully to us because, as ecologists are tirelessly telling us, the very elements that give birth to life and nurture it are themselves in peril. It is safe to say, for example, that never before has pure water seemed so precious, the water which in scripture represents the Holy Spirit. Today, therefore, it is much more helpful to explore this beautiful imagery than to analyse abstract, non-biblical phrases such as that the Holy Spirit is 'the third person of the Trinity who shares a common nature with the Father and the Son'.

GOD AND HIS WORD

The Israelites never marked time in their understanding of God. At first their God whom they came to call Yahweh ('I will be what I will be') was only one of a group of gods, a member of the pantheon. At a later date he was less a nature deity than the God of Armies who went with them to war.

In time, Israel came to see that the God who was with them in their trials and in their quest for nationhood was the only God and, therefore, the God of the whole world and all mankind. Yahweh, the Creator, was infinitely mysterious. It was idolatry to try to imagine him along the lines of the pagan baals or to think that he was confined to a particular place and at the beck and call of his worshippers. Yahweh was free; he was sovereign; he was beyond everything that could be thought or said of him. It was this last aspect of Yahweh that accounts for the frequently noted characteristic of Judaism: it is far less concerned with right thinking about God than with right conduct towards him.

Though invisible in his inmost being, Yahweh could be seen in the world he made and sustains, as well as in the salvation he brings his people. He manifests himself to everyone in the splendours of creation; and to his people in such history-making events as their exodus from bondage.

God acts and he speaks. The Hebrew word *dabar* means 'word' and 'deed'. God speaks by acting and he acts by speaking. And he himself is really present in what he says and does just as a man by his actions and his promises gives himself away to another. When a man breaks a pledge he *withdraws himself* from his promise.

God has pledged himself. He spoke his Word at creation and the life of heaven and earth began to unfold. Everything that exists discloses (or incarnates) his Word. He also gave his Word to Israel through the Sinai covenant he made with them.

Briefly, God is in his Word. It is a creative Word and a saving Word. It cannot be retracted because God is one with his Word.

GOD AND HIS SPIRIT

As there is a oneness between God and his Word, so there is a oneness between God and his Spirit. It follows that there is an intimate bond in the Bible between 'Word' and 'Spirit'.

In the creation story God is depicted as speaking or uttering his word. 'God said, "Let us make man in our image, after our likeness" ' (Gen. 1:26). This is a dialogue, but only in the sense that human beings engage in a dialogue when they speak to themselves.

As God communicates through his Word, so he is depicted in scripture as knowing himself through his Spirit. Paul expressed this Hebrew idea perfectly: 'For what person knows a man's thoughts except the spirit of the man which is in him? So also no one comprehends the thoughts of God except the Spirit of God' (1 Cor. 2:11).

The spirit is, as it were, the essential or real self. Now, God, while infinitely mysterious to men, is naturally comprehended by the depths of his own self, the Spirit. He is, as we would say, totally and lucidly self-aware. Just as God's Word is expressed in the world, so must God's Spirit be. God, his Word, his Spirit – or, better, God through his Word and Spirit – are present in everything God is and does. The whole world is a word of God filled with the Creator's inspiration.

In the beginning of things, when God is about to utter his Word, his Spirit hovers over the primeval chaos like a brooding bird. Whenever God acts or speaks, his Spirit is at work. Whenever something marvellous and new is to be done God's Spirit is at hand. When God acts graciously, whenever he brings order from 'chaos and dark night' or life from death, the Spirit is the agent of God. For the Spirit is God's very self, infinitely powerful and mysterious, poured out like pure water on the world. When the prophet (or spokesman) speaks for God, he receives God's Spirit which endows him with gifts of wisdom and understanding that do not originate in man. The prophet, having God's Spirit, speaks the Word of God. Once more, St Paul shows his Jewish caste of mind: 'We have received not the spirit of the world but the Spirit which is from God, that we might understand the gifts bestowed on us by God' (1 Cor. 2:12).

I was once interviewing Dame Sybil Thorndike, that legendary dramatic actress of the British stage, on the occasion of her ninetieth birthday. She chose to speak about her memories of Bernard Shaw. I asked her if she remembered Shaw's *Saint Joan* in which, I knew, she had starred. Her proud reply was that Shaw had written the play specially for her, and though that was nearly seventy years ago she still remembered it *word for word*. 'Bernard Shaw coached me in every line of it,' she said. Then without warning, this gracious old lady seated upright in her easy-chair, the victim of a crippling arthritis, came alive. Her eyes blazed, the white porcelain of her skin seemed trans-figured by a golden light. And she began to recite her most moving speech of long ago: 'Light your fire: do you think I dread it as much as the life of a rat in a hole? . . . Bread has no sorrow for me, and water no affliction. But to shut me from the light of the sky and the sight of the fields and flowers; to chain my feet so that I can never ride with the soldiers nor climb the hills; to make me breathe foul damp darkness, and keep me from everything that brings me back to the love of God when your wickedness and foolishness tempt me to hate him: all this is worse than the furnace in the Bible that was heated seven times. I could do without my warhorse; I could drag about in a skirt; I could let the banners and the trumpets and the knights and soldiers pass me and leave me behind as they leave the other women, if only I could still hear the wind in the trees, the larks in the sunshine, the young lambs crying through the healthy frost, and the blessed church bells that send my angel voices floating to me on the wind.' I was astounded. Sybil Thorndike was no longer herself. The spirit of Bernard Shaw was aglow in her and all the years dropped from her as she uttered lines whose every intonation and nuance of meaning belonged to the Irish author she revered.

In Israel's history there were times when individuals and the race itself spoke with the Spirit of God. They ceased for a while to be themselves. They heard other 'voices' and their wisdom was the wisdom of God himself.

GOD AND CHRIST

In John's gospel, Christ is referred to as the Word of God. In the beginning 'further back' than the beginnings of Genesis, in that beginning which was 'prior' to every beginning, the Word already was. And what God was, the Word was. And the Word became flesh.

Once again God speaks his Word with whom he is one. He makes himself known in an utterance that is decisive for mankind. In Jesus Christ, God has said all he wants to say to us. The most important Christian claim is this: to see Christ is to see God *and nothing more is needed*. In the risen Christ the fulness of God dwells in a bodily way.

He is God's Face turned in love and mercy towards us.

Jesus addressed himself to God as 'Father', 'my Father'. He was the first Jew who dared to pray to God in the familiar, everyday, Aramaic phrase, 'Abba, my Father'. Clearly, he must have been aware that he stood in a unique relationship to God in which he wanted his fellow men to share.

But if God has spoken in Christ, he must also, in Old Testament terms, have sent forth his Spirit to renew the face of the earth. The New Testament has no other terms with which to describe the mystery of Christ.

In Luke, Jesus' mother is 'overshadowed' by the Spirit. Her womb, formless and empty, resembles the chaos over which the Spirit brooded when God first uttered his creative Word. The virgin-birth is not primarily a truth about Mary but a truth about God and his Christ. A new world is beginning here; human capacities are suspended, inoperative. The second Genesis requires a power from on high, the Spirit of God.

Christian tradition saw the same Spirit working at Jesus' baptism and when he was driven into the wilderness. Jesus was about to begin his saving ministry. For that he needed to be set apart from everything evil and to receive the power and wisdom of God. This is why he goes into the desert where God awaits him; and when temptation is overcome, he sets Galilee alight in the power of the Spirit. Only the Spirit can inspire credence for such an unbelievable message: God loves the sinner.

Finally, only the Spirit of God can triumph over the scandal of the cross. Jesus died. His corpse epitomizes the sinfulness and helplessness of man. But because Jesus remained true to God to the end, the Spirit once more comes and renews the face of the earth. Jesus, crucified in weakness, is raised by the power (the Spirit) of God. The new world has already taken shape. Christ, once the Son of God in weakness, is now the Son of God in power. Now he sends upon his disciples the same Spirit of God who endowed him with the fulness of life.

THE LIFE OF THE SPIRIT

The Spirit is life. At Pentecost, he brings into being a community or storehouse of life which is the Church. Paul calls the Church Christ's body. Without the Church the risen Christ would remain invisible, unapproachable, faceless. The Church is the body and so the abiding presence of Christ. The Spirit energizes the body, gives it form, vitality, unity amid organic diversity. Without the Spirit the body of Christ would fall apart and Christ himself, for all his achievements in Galilee and on Calvary, would be a nobody in the world. But the one Spirit binds the Church, for all its faults, into one, a single fellowship of faith, love and devotion. When Adolf Hitler addressed a mass-rally the whole assembly was visibly raked by the warlike spirit of Nazism. In the film records this spirit is perceptible even now. For his part, Christ brought a Spirit of peace whose presence is no less plain: 'And he came and preached peace to you who were far off and peace to those who were near; for through him we both have access in one Spirit to the Father' (Eph. 2:17–18).

The Spirit gives to Christ's body the life of God we call 'grace' because God, by visiting us, graces us with his presence. 'If a man loves me,' Christ says, '. . . my Father will love him, and we will come to him and make our home with him' (John 14:23).

The Spirit gives a life that is beyond life, beyond the life in us that ages and dies. God's life is such that no moth can nibble it away, no burglars can steal it. Even the stealthiest burglar, Death, cannot lay his itching fingers on it. 'The kingdom of God is among you,' Jesus said. It is among us because he is among us. This is more than ever true now that he is risen and living on earth by means of the Spirit whom he sends us from God.

The Spirit consoles us because he is the abiding presence of the Lord who is himself the presence of God. The Spirit is no more a substitute for Christ than Christ is a substitute for the Father. When God the Father sent his Son to us, he himself was more intensely present to us than ever before because Christ is his final Word. In the same way, when Christ bestows his Spirit on us he is closer to us than when, in the days of his flesh, he walked the roads of Galilee. To see Christ is to see God. To experience the Spirit is to experience Christ. The Spirit is Christ himself in his fellowship with believers. This explains why Paul speaks indiscriminately of being 'in the Spirit' and 'in Christ Jesus'. It was in fact the inseparable connection of Christ and the Spirit which enabled the Church to grasp the personality of the Spirit and to read into the Jewish Bible a fresh awareness of the depths of the mystery of God.

The Spirit by which Christ lives with God is in daily communion with our spirit. He dwells in each of us, consecrating our bodies, minds and hearts. This is why for each of us the kingdom has come, the new world has begun.

PRAYING IN THE SPIRIT

Christian prayer develops and sustains the new life we have from God. Through prayer we reach out to the mystery in whom we are grounded crying, Abba! Father! But we cannot summon up the courage to address God as Father except we pray with Christ who is the throne of grace. Nor can we pray with or through Christ unless we believe that the power of God has been sent to us and his Spirit has been poured out on us. We cannot join Christ in saying 'Father', we cannot even call Christ 'Lord', unless we are taught by the Spirit and receive wisdom which is not ours but God's. 'When we cry Abba! Father! it is the Spirit himself bearing witness with our spirit that we are children of God . . . The Spirit helps us in our weakness; for we do not know how to pray as we ought, but the Spirit himself intercedes for us with sighs too deep for words' (Rom. 8:15–16, 26). Taking his cue from Paul, one author speaks movingly of the Spirit as 'the infinite Sigh of infinite Love'. Maybe a better and more Christian definition of prayer than 'the raising up of mind and heart to God' would be 'the sighing of Christ's Spirit in our spirit to God our Father'.

Recently Christendom has seen the spread of a phenomenon once confined to the Pentecostal church called 'speaking in tongues'. This movement is not so difficult to appreciate. We have all experienced moments when, as we say, words fail us. A good example of this was when the Japanese poet Teishitsu, following the custom of his people, went to look at the famous cherry blossom of Yoshino. The haiku he wrote to commemorate his visit is considered by many to be the finest possible tribute. It says nothing but it conveys a great deal:

> It was . . . It was . . . Oh!
> That's all – those blossom-covered
> hills of Yoshino.

There are times too for many Christians when articulate words seem more than usually inadequate to convey the workings of God's Spirit in our spirit. Words still suitable for everyday things, at this point cease to have meaning when applied to God. A kind of music replaces words looked at as intelligible utterances; and the singer 'sings his heart out'. Prayer becomes a melody without lyrics; the whole organism of the worshipper, body and spirit, becomes its instrument. The melody-maker is the Spirit of the Lord within.

This kind of prayer, when offered with propriety, is authorized in the New Testament itself. It seems to have been resorted to on the day of Pentecost, hence the accusation levelled against the apostles that they were drunk (Acts 2:15). Paul found examples of speaking in tongues in the church at Corinth. He did not discourage it though he was anxious not to give this spiritual inebriation too much prominence. He warned his converts that it might become an opportunity for self-indulgence and be disadvantageous to the community. He wrote: 'If I do not know the meaning of the language, I shall be a foreigner to the speaker and the speaker a foreigner to me. So with yourselves; since you are eager for manifestations of the Spirit, strive to excel in building up the Church' (1 Cor. 14:11–12). His 'more excellent way' is the way of love which taken all in all is a description of the life and character of Christ.

Paul recommends that we pray with both spirit and mind so that everybody benefits. Traditionally, the most complete expression of Christian prayer is prayer to the Father, through the Son and in the power of the Holy Spirit. By following this simple scheme every disciple of Christ, whether he understands the Athanasian Creed or not, is guaranteed that he is 'knowing' God as he wishes to be known. By it he is related immediately to God, Christ and the Spirit. He recapitulates the whole of the Bible and, therefore, the whole plan of salvation.

No study of treatises on the Trinity can replace this traditional pattern of prayer which has come down to us and which the liturgy particularly has retained. It ensures growth in the Christian spirit because it highlights the fact that there is Someone praying in us who is above us: the Holy Spirit.

Everything comes to us as a gift from the Father who speaks to us in his Word by whom he shares with us his Holy Spirit. Likewise, everything returns to the Father when the Spirit comes upon us to join us to Christ. In union with Christ we approach with childlike confidence the one whom Jesus showed to be 'the Father of mercies' (2 Cor. 1:3).

THE NEW WORLD OF THE SPIRIT

If, as I hope, the Christian teaching on God seems slightly less muddled and more truly mysterious than before, we must still face another question: Are we guilty even now of a dangerous *exclusivism*? After all, it might be argued, only Christians pray to God through Christ in the Spirit. Does it not follow that other worshippers cannot be praying in a really effective way?

My own view is that Christians are never doing what other people cannot do. They are merely doing consciously what every person must do at least implicitly if he is to be saved.

As to prayer, this is not an activity separable from life. Prayer in its most developed form is offered to God through Christ in the Spirit because *that is the general pattern of human existence*: we came from God and we journey homewards to him together with Christ and in the Spirit. Prayer should be as faithful as possible to that pattern.

But every human being, not only the Christian, is an incarnate word of the Father made in the image of the eternal Word of God and dwelt in by God's Spirit. All the time a human being is growing, whether he thinks of it or not, he is journeying to the Father with Christ. He belongs to the people of the passover simply by living and dying.

Every human being, by the same token, is a pentecostalist – none more obviously so than a new-born gurgling baby. Think of him as he is in that early phase. He looks as much like an inebriate as he is ever likely to look: bulging glassy eyes, fallen chin, drooling lips, uttering sighs and incoherent groans which mothers, who have the gift of interpreting tongues, manage to translate instinctively. Mothers understand this baby Esperanto. They appear to know when their child is saying he is hungry, thirsty, lonely, or in pain. They are at this stage the baby's God, his grace, his eucharist, his paradise.

Amusing this may be but not far-fetched. A child, as soon as he is born, commences his journey, his passover-life. He is the child of the Father and the brother of Christ; the Spirit is crying out within him for his mother's milk, for sustenance. It is the child's first prayer for life. As the baby feeds he starts to grow in Christ. If none of this is true, we would have to write off a great number of the Church's prayers, the baptismal ceremony included, as so much proud, exaggerated mother-talk.

What is said of the baby's first moments can and must be said of every human action that is not sinful: the daily grind, studying at school, the oppressiveness of commuting, the task of minding the home and bringing up the children, kissing the wife goodbye each morning, watching TV, keeping in touch with world events through the daily newspaper. We are not journeying to God through Christ in the Spirit only on those rare 'prayer-ful' moments when we are aware of doing so. We have seen already that feeding the hungry does not become a Christian act only when we realize that Christ is hungry and we are helping him. Life is not just a huge series of spiritual gaps joined together by the string of prayer.

What does prayer do, then? It sacramentalizes and celebrates life and all the actions of our day. It tells us that the good man has no gaps in his life except where he ceases to do the right thing. A prayer in the secret of the heart is a private festival of the holiness and goodness of everything that exists. It affords us an opportunity of becoming more aware of God and more grateful to him for his goodness and his Fatherly nearness, the appreciation of which is Christianity's greatest contribution to religion.

People who do not consciously pray are not necessarily evil; they may refuse on principle to pray to a God in whom they cannot believe. But they are certainly deprived of a special kind of peace and joy. Prayer is sometimes called 're-collection'. This word conveys the idea that in prayer we gather up the scattered fragments of our day and bring them back like sheep to the fold. In this way, our life acquires a sense of wholeness. We see vividly that nothing we did, enjoyed, suffered, has been wasted.

In prayer, too, we are, in Eliot's words, looking for 'the still point of the turning world'. We would like, in our small way, to go beyond those distracting moments 'in and out of time'.

> But to apprehend
> The point of intersection of the timeless
> With time is an occupation for the saint.[7]

Perhaps. But amateurs too may try their hand at it!

Prayer is communing with the Spirit. It involves, in the colourful English phrase, 'having a Breather', getting our Breath back, being given divine re-Spiration. Thomas Aquinas has an even more evocative description of prayer: *recreatio mentis in Deum*, the recreation of the soul in God. Prayer, he suggests, far from being first and foremost a solemn duty is the playtime of the spirit. Those who do not pray are missing out on this exceptional playful repose and recreation. But again let it be said, their lives are still passover-lives. Whenever they love, they, like the Good Samaritan, pass over a little more from death to life in company with Christ. All this is the work of the Spirit.

The Spirit is deeply involved in creation and re-creation. By bringing the whole world into contact with God through Christ he introduces mankind to the glorious environment of the new world in which God's children are privileged to live. This is why the action of the Spirit is described in scripture in terms of the cherished elements of this world which he has set in order, purified, elevated.

In the new world the Spirit is for everyone the source of life and joy. He is the fountain of water, the life-giving breath, the liberating wind, the consoling and consuming fire, the oil that gladdens and consecrates the heart of man, the Dove of divine forgiveness, the first fruits of the land.

Discussion questions

Is it true that the doctrine of God, Christ and the Spirit has become for many Christians more of a muddle than a mystery? To what extent has a shift in language contributed to the muddle? Are we entitled to alter traditional terminology when we find it unhelpful or confusing?

What is meant by 'Word' and 'Spirit' in scripture? What examples are there in our language comparable to biblical usage?

Does the Church show signs of being lived in by the Spirit? Does your own family, your own parish?

Is there one definition of Christian prayer you like more than others? What is it? Can you defend its adequacy?

Why does the Church in the liturgy pray most usually to the Father, through the Son and in the Spirit? Do you pray like this? If not, why not? If so, what benefits do you derive from it?

Do you find prayer hard? If so, why? Should prayer be hard? What do you hope to get out of prayer; and put into it? Do you pray much during the day? Today, for instance? What evoked prayer in you? Do you tend to think the hours are wasted when you don't pray? Do you find prayer-ful people out of this world or in the thick of it?

Do you agree that even non-Christians must approach God through Christ in the Spirit? Can non-believers be filled with Christ's Spirit? Who is the most Spirit-filled person you know? What qualities do you most admire in this person?

2. *Water*

Spirit of Jesus, living Water,
In our dry hearts, a secret spring.
We'll never thirst but drink for ever from you
    Deep within.

THE SPLENDOUR OF WATER

'We want lots and lots of hot water.' In the old Hollywood films this was always the cry that presaged the arrival of a child. Knowing I was born by candlelight on a dark November evening, I have often wondered whether it was hard for the midwife to wash and handle me when I was born.

When we are born and when we die we are cleansed with water. It was always a childhood source of magic to me that my mother's mother had the role of 'laying out' the dead of her immediate locality. She told me how she washed their white bodies and crossed their arms and smudged their eyelids into place and bound their heads with a bandage so the chin was set in an expression of peace. I think my grandmother may have been chosen because she was so trusted and so gentle; and she gave her services free.

Between the twin-decencies done to us at birth and death, how often we need to wash and refresh ourselves with water.

Perhaps water is too easily available for us in the West to cherish it as we should. This is why the precariousness of our existence is hidden from us, the basic truth that without water there is no bread and wine and that when we are too dry we cannot swallow whatever food we have. The very expression 'on tap' is used to indicate a commodity or service we need never go without. In all my life I can only recall one day of intolerable thirst. I was a sixteen-year-old army cadet taking part in manœuvres. The sun beat down on us mercilessly. Three of our comrades died of sunstroke that day. For the rest of my life, my thirst has been easily assuaged; though I have not blessed God as I should.

In addition to its usefulness for washing and drinking, water has been for me as for everyone a source of special delight. It was a puddle when I was young and not so young to splash through; a brook full of minnows and leeches to wade in against the sternest parental advice; a winter's pond for skating on; a broad stream in summer almost choked with watercress; a winding river on which in adolescence we rowed or inexpertly guided our punts. And the sea. I once heard a Greek cry, 'Thálassa', 'The Sea!' and it seemed the loveliest sound I had ever heard. It evoked the beauty and mystery of the sea which is the image of God, 'always moving and always still'. My mother told me that when she first saw the sea she did not realize she was looking at water at all but thought it a huge, grey sheet of corrugated iron!

Water arouses mixed feelings in us. Witness so many children's early unwillingness to bathe or try to swim. This is because water is at once the gentlest and most ruthless of the elements. It can give life and it can take it away. It depends, too, upon the water's mood whether we are attracted to it or repelled by it.

In any case, water, life's earliest home for both the individual and the race, is the most vital of earth's gifts. Polluted water, as we are beginning to realize almost too late, is an abomination like salt that is no longer salty. Without clean water the cycles of nature cease to turn; and everything withers and everything dies.

ISRAEL'S THEOLOGY OF WATER

For Israel, God, by dispensing or withholding water, controls the life of the world. Water is God's creature. Through the perforated dome of heaven descends the nightly dew, and through it the rain pours down to bring the late and early harvests. Beneath the earth there is another vast expanse of water from which come the fountains and the streams.

> Thou makest springs gush forth in the valleys;
>   they flow between the hills . . .
> From thy lofty abode thou waterest the mountains;
>   the earth is satisfied with the fruit of thy work.
> Thou dost cause the grass to grow for the cattle,
>   and plants for man to cultivate,
> that he may bring forth food from the earth,
> and wine to gladden the heart of man (Ps. 104:10, 13–15).

For a God-centred people like Israel, water becomes an eloquent symbol of the relationship between God and man. God is all-powerful and man is so needy that without water he, his animals and his crops all die. Water expresses the daily, all-pervasive dependence of man on his creator. God is himself the fountain of water. In Jeremiah, God complains of two evils committed by his people:

> They have forsaken me, the fountain of living waters,
>   and hewed out cisterns for themselves,
> broken cisterns, that can hold no water (2:13).

Even the cleansing aspect of water is transformed into ritual or 'purification'. In the first place, hospitality is a sacred duty; the feet of visitors must be cleansed of their journey's stains. But there is also the symbolic cleansing of

hands about to touch food and of vessels used at meals.
True, at times this practice became too elaborate, too
superficial, indeed a substitute for genuine personal holiness. This is the only reason why Jesus, a pious Jew, found
it reprehensible. In itself, as is proven by the Christian
sacrament of baptism, outer cleansing can become a pleasing
sign of inner purity. But always it is inner purity that God
is seeking. In Isaiah, he says to his people:

> Wash yourselves; make yourselves clean;
>   remove the evil of your doings from before my eyes . . .
> though your sins are like scarlet,
>   they shall be as white as snow;
> though they are red like crimson,
>   they shall become like wool (1:16, 18).

On a broader scale, Israel recounted one tale (a myth)
in which the whole world was purified of its iniquity
by means of a Flood and another (a saga) in which
the Egyptian oppressors were swallowed up in the Red
Sea.

Plainly, Israel, too, had mixed feelings about water! It
could become either a token of God's blessing or his
punishment. He gave his people water in the desert when
Moses, at his bidding, struck a rock with his rod. But there
were times when, in his wrath, God forged the skies into
iron and the earth's crust into brass (Lev. 26:19). Then
Israel's only hope was in prayer and penitence.

However, the ultimate Jewish vision in which water was
prominent was one of joy. Israel looked forward as in a
dream to the 'last times', a paradisal state in which the
original lost, well-watered garden of delights was entirely
restored. Mankind (Adam) had been thrust out of Eden
where rivers freely flowed and been forced to till a barren
land in which thorns and thistles multiplied. But one day
God promises:

I will make them walk by brooks of water,
   in a straight path in which they shall not stumble
(Jer. 31:9).

Why, the very desert will become a paradise:

I will pour water on the thirsty land,
   and streams on the dry ground;
I will pour my Spirit upon your descendants,
   and my blessing on your offspring.
They shall spring up like grass amid waters,
   like willows by flowing streams (Is. 44:3–4).

I will make the wilderness a pool of water,
   and the dry land springs of water.
I will put in the wilderness the cedar,
   the acacia, the myrtle, and the olive;
I will set in the desert the cypress,
   the plane and the pine together (Is. 41:18–19).

One needs to see the wickedness of the desert at close quarters to appreciate this vision with its emphasis on the preciousness of water.

A WATERLESS WASTE

I first met the desert twenty years ago. It was a brief and casual encounter. We were motoring from Damascus, east of the river, to Jerusalem. We barely touched the fringes of the Jordanian desert but it was the height of summer. In that cauldron, without assistance the bravest and strongest die within two days after insane babblings. Though our car had no air-conditioning, it was nevertheless better to keep the windows closed, so hot was the desert air. Imperious camels padded by, driven by Bedouins. Sand permeated everything, locked suitcases included, lodging even in the crevices and folds of the skin. We drove for hours through this treeless, airless, odourless waste.

It was this memory, I believe, that made it impossible for me years later to refuse a plea for money made by a pauper of the Far East. He wrote to me: 'I live in your shade.' Despite the unrighteous anger aroused in me by the demands of one so much poorer than myself, I had to help him. His simple words made me see that I was the solitary tree in his desert. Without me and the pittance I gave he would frizzle in the sun.

Recently I had lunch with a friend, Geoffrey Moorhouse. Geoffrey had sent me in advance the manuscript of his best-selling book, *The Fearful Void*,[8] the astonishing story of how he had attempted to cross the Sahara by camel from Mauritania on the Atlantic coast to the Nile.

The hours passed quickly and quietly between us. Geoffrey, brown-eyed, with drooping sandy moustache and receding hair slanted sideways across his head, seemed scarcely the typical explorer. He relived without obvious emotion the two thousand miles he had covered, the last three hundred or so almost entirely on foot across the blistering sand.

Like T. E. Lawrence and Sir Richard Burton before him, Geoffrey Moorhouse had been as intrigued by the interior journey he was about to make as by the physical hardships to be endured. In the event, he hated the sores that broke out on his body, the bizarre food, the thirst, the dysentery, the perpetual lice, the burning sun by day, the strange and awful frigidity of night. (I remembered the whimsical Arabic saying: the Sahara is a cold country where it is very hot in the sun.) But there were compensations: the mystery of the desert, freedom from ties, the appalling nearness of God.

Experts had warned Geoffrey never to venture into the desert alone. He soon realized that this was not merely a piece of practical advice – though it is true he would never have been able by himself to round up the camels and saddle them with all the equipment four times a day. Nor could he have braved the elements when he was ill. But there was, besides all this, the sheer massive, silent presence of the seas of sand and the sky. Alone in such wildness a man could hardly carry on.

In the desert, Geoffrey explained, no one travels as the crow flies. Wells and oases dictate directions. At every stop, the *guerbas* (or water-skins) have to be replenished. Around an oasis there might be a splash of greenery, trees and rushes where donkeys, camels, herons and egrets could make their home. Usually the water in the wells – often no more than holes in the ground – was mixed with mud and urine and tufts of camel-dung. Even so it was precious. It meant the difference between living and dying.

There was one occasion when his mischievous and melancholy companion Ould Mohammed had foolishly spilt the contents of a vital *guerba* into the sand. Geoffrey thought there was nothing left but to wait for the end. When, after a long interval, Ould Mohammed surprisingly reappeared, he offered Geoffrey a cooking pot half-full of water with the words, '*Shrabt, shrabt.*' 'Drink.' The water was mixed with all manner of filth, morsels of rice, strands of hair from the *guerba*, camel-dung. Yet it smelt cool and fresh; and as the vessel slanted towards him Geoffrey thought it 'the most wonderful thing that had happened to me in my life'.

There was another occasion when death from thirst seemed imminent. This time it was a little boy who brought him a bowl with some water the colour of diluted blood. To Geoffrey this was the most beautiful thing in the world, more beautiful than the stained-glass of Chartres, a fugue by Bach, the embrace of the woman he loved, the sweet adulation of his son.

Geoffrey Moorhouse gave the most eloquent appraisal of

water I have heard. Afterwards, some words of Jesus took
on a deeper meaning: 'Whoever gives to one of these little
ones even a cup of cold water because he is a disciple, truly,
I say to you, he shall not lose his reward' (Matt. 10:42).

JESUS IN THE DESERT

Jesus went into the desert. He was driven there by the
Spirit to seek a more intense awareness of his forthcoming
mission. He had been baptized by one who described himself as a voice howling in the wilderness; he had taken his
place among malefactors on the banks of the Jordan. Now
he leaves behind the waters and the green banks and goes
into the emptiness to look for God.

Israel had lived in the desert for forty years. They were
years of fear, temptation, backsliding and occasional
despair. God was testing Israel to find out what was in her
heart and whether she would keep his commandments.
Moses, the leader of the Israelites, had spent forty days and
nights on the side of a mountain without eating or drinking
so as to be worthy to receive the law of the Lord on their
behalf.

Jesus, too, is a law-giver and leader. And no coward.
He confronts the dreaded desert, going without food and
drink for forty days and nights. Significantly, he dares to
venture into the desert alone.

Everything there is exaggerated, both landscape and
skyscape. The sun is hotter, the night air colder, the wind
more venomous, the moon and stars bigger and brighter.
There are beasts within and without. Terrors are nearer
and intenser, as near and pressing as dehydrated flesh is to
the bone. And mirages appear, false projections of what lies
ahead, mirages of food, wonders, world-conquest.

Jesus did not wilt under the pressures of his long interior
journey. He looked steadfastly into the big eyes of God and

knew that he himself was nothing. The desert sands are always virginal; they are open to every possibility. Empty, unscarred, unchanging from age to age. In the desert man's achievements do not count. He stands there as in a vast temple without walls or roof or monuments or paving, listening to the voice of God in the wind. He is reduced to the bare essentials of being a man: body and spirit, pain and longings, temptations like sword-thrusts and dreams racing through the soul like a storm.

Jesus underwent the crucifixion of the desert before angels came and ministered to him. God mercifully came and wrapped him round with the consolation of his Spirit.

But the desert had marked Jesus for ever. He emerged as a black tangled 'root out of a thirsty ground, without beauty or comeliness'. He looked like any victim of drought or famine in one of today's tormented lands. Here was God's Suffering and Unprofitable Servant. Behold the Lamb of God.

Through it all he had not bartered his soul for food and drink; he had not forsaken the Fountain of living water.

THE MAN WITH WATER

The fourth evangelist recounts the story of the woman at the well (John 4). Every day this Samaritan had to go to Jacob's well to fill her bucket. The well was deep, and letting down the bucket and pulling it up and carrying it home – that was hard work in the sun. When the bucket had been emptied she was obliged to return again and again, day after day. It was the only way to live.

It was midday when Jesus, hot and tired after a long journey, sat down beside the well and asked for a drink. She was surprised that a Jew should ask a Samaritan heretic for a drink. He said: 'If you knew the gift of God and who it is who is saying to you, "Give me a drink," you would

have asked him, and he would have given you living water'
(4:10). Jesus promises not dead water from a well but living
water, running, bubbling, flowing water.

The Samaritan woman is perplexed: the Jew has no
bucket and the well is deep. Perhaps he is only making fun
of her; he can tell from her solitariness she is an outcast
even among her own people. But Jesus is speaking of the
Spirit whom he offers to the lost of the lost. Water drawn
from the well is used up very soon; then the long journey
back to fill up the bucket again. Jesus has other water to
give, water that will go on satisfying for ever. A man has
only to drink of this water and goodbye thirst. The human
heart of itself is a barren place. Jesus offers to bestow on all
believers a secret interior spring, a fountain of water
bubbling up to eternal life: the Holy Spirit.

Later, on the last and great day of the desert festival
called Tabernacles, when water-libations were made, Jesus
stood up and cried: 'If any one thirst, let him come to me;
and let him who believes in me drink. As the scripture has
said, "Out of his heart shall flow rivers of living water".' The
evangelist explains that Jesus was referring to the Spirit
who was still not given to believers. 'As yet the Spirit had
not been given, because Jesus was not yet glorified' (John
7:37–39).

It was another hot midday when Jesus' hour of glory
came. He was fixed upon his cross. Surrounded once more
by malefactors, he underwent his second baptism, the
baptism of death.

With an animal cry: 'I am thirsty!' He is thoroughly
poor, needy, desolate, at the end of all human resources.
This dried-up Christ is about to give the never-failing waters
of the Spirit.

A soldier takes his lance and opens Christ's heart. It is
as when Moses, taking a rod, struck the rock in the desert
so that water sprang from it. Water springs from the heart

of Christ. 'Out of *his* heart shall flow rivers of living water.'
He had to go away so that the Spirit could come.

WATER IN THE WILDERNESS

Life in the biblical imagery is a journey through the desert.
The end and aim of it is God. We must seek God more
eagerly than thirsty men seek water. God is the source of
life, the only fountain men can drink from.

> O God, you are my God, for you I long;
> for you my soul is thirsting.
> My body pines for you
> like a dry, weary land without water (Ps. 63:1).

> Like the deer that yearns
> for running streams,
> so my soul is yearning
> for you, my God.
> My soul is thirsting for God,
> the God of my life;
> when can I enter and see
> the face of God? (Ps. 42:1–2)

Christ, by dying for us, put God's Spirit within us. Now
we can travel through the desert *unafraid*. We can throw
away the heavy *guerbas* that were continually slowing us
down. No need to change direction to visit wells and oases
where the water is perhaps mixed in any case with desert
sand and camel-dung.

Within the believer is pure water bubbling up from the
interior fountain which is God's Holy Spirit. The believer
has life within him, life in such abundance he can afford
to share it freely with others. In him and around him the
wilderness becomes a pool of water; the cedar, acacia,
myrtle and the olive grow. The human heart becomes a
paradise.

And there is no end to the dream, for Christ says: 'It is done! I am the Alpha and the Omega, the beginning and the end. To the thirsty I will give from the fountain of the water of life without payment' (Rev. 21:6).

WHERE THE SPRINGS OF WATER ARE

I said it was a dream. Of course. Life cannot go on without dreams: day-dreams as well as the dreams of night. Men need dreams as much as they need bread. In this instance, the dream only expresses what *everyone* basically experiences and yearns for. It was disclosed to Christians most forcefully in the self-sacrificing death of Jesus Christ.

'I've had enough. I can't go on. Not another step.' Where is the man who has never felt like that? Then, unexpectedly perhaps, someone speaks a thoughtful word, or expresses gratitude for a kindness done a long while ago, or simply smiles. That person is a channel of new life and strength. He proffers the needed cup of cold water which enables the weary traveller to journey on a little further.

Or it may be a man has quarrelled with his wife. After a prolonged internal dialogue which he eventually loses, he says to himself: 'I was wrong. It *was* my fault. I shouldn't have pretended she was to blame. I'd better say I'm sorry.' Just then his wife comes into the room and tells him *she* is sorry. Fresh water washes over his heart. He cannot forgive himself and yet he is forgiven. He is cleansed.

Or a woman has a mongoloid child. For long spells she finds the happening humiliating, depressing, exhausting. Her only solace is her husband. He is always there: an unfailing fountain of love and understanding.

Someone might want to say at this point: Up till now, you have been talking about the waters of the Spirit. But in those three examples you have turned to *human* acts of kindness and generosity.

Naturally. God always acts through men. That is what 'incarnation' means. It was only through the pierced heart of a Man that the waters of the Spirit flowed freely into the world. It is wrong not reverent to try and establish a kind of rivalry between God and man. As if, say, the invention of penicillin were somehow less holy than a miraculous cure at a sacred shrine. As if, man in his inventions and God in his miracles, each acts alone. In fact, without God's inspiration there would be no human inventiveness, just as without man's faith there would be no miracles.

God loves us in the Man, Jesus Christ. God loves us in the love we have for one another. When, for example, a husband loves his wife he is already loving God. Prayer at the moment of an embrace might diminish rather than deepen his love. Sometimes we are distracted *in* our prayers and sometimes, as in this case, *by* them. Bonhoeffer wrote: 'Speaking frankly, to long for the transcendent when you are in your wife's arms is, to put it mildly, a lack of taste, and it is certainly not what God expects of us. We ought to find God and love him in the blessings he sends us. If he pleases to grant us some overwhelming earthly bliss, we ought not to try and be more religious than God himself.'[9]

A person who tries to be more religious than God himself is suffering from the malady called 'religiosity'. Not content with the inherent sacredness of life, he feels he has to gild it with 'super-natural' or 'spiritual' motives to justify him sleeping with his wife. He may even pray while so doing, in order, as it were, to bring God into the act. There is no need for such solicitude. God is already there but not *in addition to* the love of man and wife. He is there *as* the love of man and wife.

Bonhoeffer also pinpointed another, more frightening error of religiosity:

Nothing can fill the gap when we are away from those

we love, and it would be wrong to try and find anything.
We must simply hold out and win through. That sounds
very hard at first, but at the same time it is a great
consolation, since leaving the gap unfilled preserves the
bonds between us. It is nonsense to say that God fills
the gap: he does not fill it, but keeps it empty so that
our communion with another may be kept alive, even
at the cost of pain.[10]

I like this passage more than I can say. God would not
be God if he required us to love him more by loving our
dear ones less. Our love of God, I said, is not an addition
to our love of one another, but neither is it a substitute for
loving them. We cannot turn from our loved ones to God
nor from God to our loved ones. Either we love everyone
in loving God and God in loving everyone – or there is no
love in us. 'If any one says, "I love God," and hates his
brother, he is a liar; for he who does not love his brother
whom he has seen, cannot love God whom he has not seen'
(1 John 4:20).

Sometimes we focus expressly on the divine depths of
human love, on that Love underlying everything (1 John
4:8). That is formal prayer. For the believer, it is a source
of peace and joy. But whether we notice him or not, God
is present all the same – and he is often more intensely
present for our *not* noticing him.

God acts through Christ his representative. Christ acts
through all people who love their fellows. In the desert of
life there are many who – though they do not know it and
would not claim it for themselves – are 'other Christs'. They
become fountains of water to many a weary traveller. Their
tenderness and concern give to those they help a sense of
holiness, a taste of that Love in which all life is rooted. In
them, the thirsty discover 'a spring of water bubbling up
to eternal life'.

Discussion questions

In how many ways have you made use of water today? Can you recall an incident in your life which made you especially appreciative of water? Are you the kind of person who tends to pollute water and if so what does this tell you about yourself?

What religious significance is given to water in Judaism? in Christianity? in any other major religion in which water has a sacramental value?

Which passage in the Bible relating to water impresses you most and why?

Have you today given to, or received from a fellow human being a 'cup of cold water'?

Which person of your acquaintance would you say has most evidently within him a spring of water bubbling up into eternal life?

What does the fourth evangelist mean by the words: 'As yet the Spirit had not been given, because Jesus was not yet glorified'? (John 7:39)

What connection is there between Christ's promise of a spring of water bubbling up to eternal life (John 4:14) and the water flowing from his side (John 19:34) when he was crucified?

What are the things people most thirst for today? Are these things worthy of the children of God?

3. *Wind*

Spirit of Jesus, Wind from heaven,
Where you come from we can't see.
But like the wind that blows upon the waters
We are free.

THE BLOWING OF THE WIND

Pope John, when asked the purpose of the Second Vatican Council soon to transform the Church, is alleged to have opened the window of his room in a prophetic gesture.

Mind you, those who have lived for any length of time in Rome will wonder where the Pope expected the fresh air to come from. The stagnant heat of the city for large stretches of the year is almost unbearable; and when the south-east wind blows from Africa, it is as if vultures are spreading their wings on every pavement and rooftop.

There used to be an old Scots curial cardinal resident in Rome who had the reputation of being a very understanding confessor. He waived aside all his penitents' offences with a characteristic gruff remark: 'It's this damned *scirocco*.' After such princely exoneration, the formal absolution on behalf of Higher Authority seemed superfluous. One of the cardinal's chief attractions for English penitents was his frequently repeated convictions: 'Americans can commit mortal sin. Even Italians. The Scots have a kind of flair for it. But Englishmen, never! Their motives are always too mixed.' Such wisdom was in itself a breath of *aria fresca* in that heat-clogged city.

Remember the old prints of maps on which the winds were represented with a benign, sunny face or with cheeks billowing with anger, about to exhale explosively. People knew exactly what face to fix on 'the winds of change' which a former British Prime Minister spoke of as blowing across the continent of Africa.

Wind, like nature's other elements, is not without its perplexities. It brings the rain clouds without which earth is a waterless waste; but sometimes it gathers itself into a frenzy that devastates the land and turns the sea into an open grave. It has a voice like a living thing, a voice of astonishing range. It sighs and whispers and whines; it cries and it howls. It is like the voice of the world.

Ask anyone who has spent long periods in the desert what are its most characteristic sounds. The answer invariably is: the slop of water in the *guerbas* and the whistle of the wind.

In *The Heart Of The Hunter*, Laurens van der Post tells of the reverence which the Bushman of the Kalahari has for the wind. He is so intimate with the wind as to feel he is *inside* it. 'The wind was the ancient first urge of life from long before his own personal being, travelling on and on when the dust had been laid over his last spoor, for new acts of creation beyond.'[11] The Bushman relies on the wind to blow away his footprints when he dies so no one is under the illusion that he is living on. He trusts that when he breathes his last, his corporeal wind will join with the great wind that fashions the clouds without which life could not continue on earth.

Of course, the wind in the desert can suffocate or drown the traveller with sand, but there are gentler, purer moments, one of which Lawrence describes in *The Seven Pillars Of Wisdom*. He was once taken by Arab guides to visit a Roman palace-ruin in North Syria. The building clay had been kneaded not with water but with the oils of flowers, jessamine, violet, rose. All went sniffing from room to room like dogs. 'But at last,' wrote Lawrence,

'Dahoum drew me: "Come and smell the very sweetest scent of all", and we went into the main lodging, to the gaping window sockets of the eastern face, and there drank with open mouths of the effortless, empty, eddyless winds of the desert, throbbing past. That slow breath had been born somewhere beyond the distant Euphrates and had dragged its way across many days and nights of dead grass, to its first obstacle, the man-made walls of our broken palace. About them it seemed to fret and linger, murmuring in baby-speech. "This," they told me, "is the best: it has no taste." My Arabs were turning their backs on perfumes and luxuries to choose the things in which mankind had no share or part.'[12]

ISRAEL'S THEOLOGY OF THE WIND

Israel had not opted for the harshness of the desert – they informed Moses in the clearest terms that they were pining for the perfumes and luxuries of Egypt – but theirs was a desert creed nonetheless. It was in every sense a wind-swept creed.

In their first credal myth, Yahweh is depicted as walking with the Man and the Woman in the cool of the day, when the wind freshened the trees in the garden (Gen. 3). It was with a strong wind that God made the waters of the Flood subside (Gen. 8:1). At the Exodus, the Red Sea parted, enabling Israel to escape from bondage, when the winds came: 'At the blast of thy nostrils, the waters piled up' (Exod. 15:8). It was the wind that brought quails from the sea when the Israelites were hungry in the desert (Num. 11:31).

But the wind could destroy as well. The prophets described defeat and exile in precisely these terms. 'The Lord removed them with his fierce blast in the day of the east wind' (Is. 27:8). This dry hot wind is the merciless

army that is smiting them: 'A hot wind from the bare
heights in the desert toward the daughter of my people,
not to winnow or cleanse, a wind too full for this comes
for me. Now it is I who speak in judgement upon them'
(Jer. 4:11–12).

Jeremiah insists that the wind of destruction comes from
God. More, God himself comes riding on the wild, gossamer
wings of the wind:

> He rode on a cherub and flew;
> he was seen upon the wings of the wind (2 Sam. 22:11).

Lord, the Psalmist cries, thou art he

> who makest the clouds thy chariot,
>   who ridest on the wings of the wind,
> who makest the winds thy messengers,
>   fire and flame thy ministers (Ps. 104:3–4).

The ambiguities, I repeat, are endless. The wind enables
the farmer to winnow his wheat; it sweeps away the foul,
stale air; it spreads across the land the perfumes of spring
flowers so that Yahweh, the Beloved, is enticed to visit his
garden, Israel:

> Awake, O north wind
>   and come, O south wind!
> Blow upon my garden,
>   let its fragrance be wafted abroad.
> Let my beloved come to his garden
>   and eat its choicest fruits (Cant. 4:16).

Yet the wind can no more be tamed or harnessed than
the sea. It is too capricious by far. At times, the most anyone
can do is try to hide from its wrath. The Israelites used to
say of a good man or an upright king: 'He is a hiding-place
from the wind.' Without question, a sturdy and resourceful
fellow!

Wind is unpredictable and blind and empty. Men who listened to false prophets were said to 'feed on wind', that is, on words that are only words, on senseless vibrations of air. The aimless scurrying of the wind was, for Job, a perfect image of the life of man, 'a hurrying from nothing to nothing' (7:7). Ecclesiastes also saw in the ceaseless veerings of the wind from north to south, from south to north, a sign that the whole of life is vanity. There is no pattern to it, no discernible logic. What in the end are the wages of the evil and the good but the wind?

Such images appear and reappear in Jewish literature throughout the Old Testament period. Humans are helpless like leaves or chaff before the storm. Our iniquities like the wind have carried us away. The sinner, having sown the wind, will reap the whirlwind. And Jeremiah, in a telling phrase, warns the unfaithful leaders of Israel what is going to happen to them: 'The wind shall shepherd all you shepherds' (22:22). They will all be blown together for punishment, a foolish flock of shepherds.

WIND FROM ABOVE

In John 3, Nicodemus, a ruler of the Jews, comes to Jesus by night. The night symbolizes for John the darkness of ignorance and sin which Christ the Light of the World was destined to dispel. This was the night into which Judas, the son of perdition, melted when he slipped away from the Last Supper to betray his Master. The same night enveloped the world when Jesus was crucified.

Jesus tells old Nicodemus that he must be born from above if he is to see God's kingdom. Nicodemus, a master in Israel, fails to understand. Can a man be born when he is old? Can he return a second time into his mother's womb and be born again? Jesus' reply is that everyone, even the old, must be born again of water and the Spirit. Rebirth is the condition of entry into God's kingdom. The first birth is from flesh to flesh; the second is from Spirit to spirit. By this new birth from above a man is born of the Spirit; he *is* spirit.

Jesus adds: 'Do not be surprised when I say, "You must be born from above". The wind blows where it wills, and you hear the sound of it, but you do not know whence it comes or whither it goes; so it is with everyone who is born of the Spirit' (3:7–8).

In this story, Jesus speaks of the wind, firstly because in both Greek and Hebrew the same word stands for 'spirit' and 'wind'; secondly because in Jewish tradition, as we saw, the wind is an element beyond human calculation or control.

The wind is mysterious; it comes from above, from the upper reaches of the sky, though its exact origin is unknown. And it comes whenever it pleases without consulting man. The Spirit (the Wind) of God is far more mysterious; its origin is heaven, the home of God. No one has come from there except Christ and the Spirit whom he promised to send. The Spirit comes effortlessly from God's high place to man's low place. It comes whenever it pleases. It is invisible; but the sound of it can be heard, the strength of it can be felt, even in the blackest night.

The Spirit, the Wind from heaven, is essentially free. We speak of being 'free as air', 'free as the wind'. We can prove it on any blustery March day by watching the patterns it makes on a pond or a lake. No one can forecast the breathing of the wind, the path it will follow, the spume it will toss. Or simply go into the garden and try to catch the wind in your hands. You cannot imprison the wind. It eludes all its would-be gaolers.

In this story, Jesus is using the humanly unpredictable movements of the wind to illustrate that God's own Spirit is at work in the world. The Spirit is freedom and life. He comes and goes when and where he pleases. The wind that blows freely on water and trees and grassland is but a feeble image of God's freedom.

FREE AS THE WIND

According to the poetry of the New Testament, the wind of heaven is within us. Our hearts become a new environment, a heaven in which the Wind of God comes and sings. He is free, joyful, buoyant. within us. We are the Wind-swept heaven of God. Christians, like Christ, are called to be freer than the wind. God's freedom within us sets us free in a new way. In baptism, we are not only born of the Spirit, we *are* spirit (John 3:6) Like the Bushman of the Kalahari we feel we are inside the wind, sharing in its life-giving properties. We *are* the wind, hence freedom, peace, joy, lightness of heart.

But what are we freed from and freed for?

Firstly, the Spirit frees us from our sins, from the heavy hand of past wrongdoing. He frees us, too, from the compulsive need to sin; we are no longer slaves to sin. 'For you did not receive the spirit of slavery to fall back into fear, but you have received the spirit of sonship' (Rom. 8:15). The son is a free-man like his father. The Spirit frees us from death. Naturally, we will die but death will not be a 'dead-end', a cul-de-sac. What Augustine said of his mother should be true of all Christians: 'She died but not miserably. She died but not altogether.' There is a Latin inscription which reads: *Mors Christi mors mortis mihi.* 'Christ's death is my death's death.' On account of the Spirit who joins us to Christ, death will only mean that we will be more open than before to the charity of Love which is God.

The most important thing from which the Spirit frees us is ourselves. The most impenetrable of sins is self-righteous-

ness, self-justification. In Jesus' parable of the Pharisee and
the Publican, the Pharisee was not a sensuous man, a man
who indulged 'the flesh' as we understand the term. Today
his name would never appear in the scandal columns of
the press. Yet in the scriptural sense the Pharisee was a
man of flesh because he trusted in himself and in his own
resources, instead of in God. This is to say he trusted in
human weakness (flesh) and not in God (strength, power,
Spirit).

The Pharisee lurks in every man. Someone remarked
that the usual reaction to Jesus' parable is, 'Thank God,
I'm not like that Pharisee.' Our purpose in prayer often
seems to be to reproduce in ourselves the very sentiments
Jesus condemned in the Pharisee. We are determined to
impress on God that we are not in all respects unprofitable
servants but really rather admirable. In *The Four Loves*, C.
S. Lewis admits that the believer's confession of unworthi
ness sometimes sounds like the self-depreciation of the
Chinese gentleman when he calls himself 'this coarse and
illiterate person'. But C. S. Lewis thinks it is more than that.
It is the attempt, however imperfectly expressed, to get
right our fundamental relationship to God. It entails a
constant struggle:

No sooner do we believe that God loves us than there is
an impulse to believe that he does so, not because he is
Love, but because we are intrinsically lovable. The
pagans obeyed this impulse unabashed; a good man was
'dear to the gods' because he was good. We, being better
taught, resort to subterfuge. Far be it from us to think
that we have virtues for which God could love us. But
then, how magnificently we have repented! As Bunyan
says, describing his first and illusory conversion, 'I
thought there was no man in England that pleased God
better than I.' Beaten out of this, we next offer our own

humility to God's admiration. Surely he'll like *that*? Or if not that, our clear-sighted recognition that we still lack humility. Thus, depth beneath depth and subtlety within subtlety, there remains some lingering idea of our own, our very own, attractiveness.[13]

The Spirit, ideally speaking, has freed us from this endless, suffocating task of justifying ourselves by joining us to Christ who is our wisdom and justification (1 Cor. 1:30). The question is not, 'Will God accept me and my gifts?' but 'Will I accept God's gifts to me of which Christ is the first?'

The Johannine imagery of the Wind from heaven expresses brilliantly the graciousness and sovereignty of God, both of which are central to the gospel message. The wind comes not because we have bidden it but because it wants to (John 3:8). Paradoxically, the Spirit comes to set us free *for service*: we must serve others as Christ serves us. This is the test of whether we are really Christians: do we help others as Christ helps us? There can be no other genuine criterion of whether Christ's Spirit is blowing in our lives and in the lives of our fellow men.

WHERE THE WIND BLOWS

Once again it is evident that Christianity is not talking in riddles. No human being is completely unaware of the spiritual process of 'going out of himself', of being liberated from his selfish self. 'I didn't dream I could do it!' 'I didn't know it was in me.' 'This time I've surpassed myself.' 'Did I do that?' We surprise ourselves. We are lifted up and carried along as by a wind whose origin we cannot fix, whose mechanism we cannot see or hear.

The mother of a family acquires a stamina and selflessness her own mother would never have thought possible; she gives uncomplainingly and without thought of recompense. A selfish husband agrees for his wife's sake to have a child though it means a complete change in the personal, economic and social habits to which he is deeply attached. A son goes on revering his bungling, alcoholic father, knowing he has been failed by him constantly; in the strangest of strange mutations, he learns to father his own father.

Through everyone's life a mysterious and unpredictable wind is blowing, driving away the stale air, dislodging us from the narrow alleyways in which our spirit tends to get wedged. Sometimes, maybe most times, we hang on for 'dear death', but there must be few men in whom the Spirit is resisted always. Such moments are clearly recognizable because we do not know ourselves. They prove we are made not in the image of an idol but in the image of God.

However, only the person who has achieved some kind of *permanent* inner liberation can be the champion of the oppressed. Christ himself underwent an apprenticeship of thirty years for his life's work: to help the down-trodden, to set prisoners free. He would have recognized a good disciple in Mahatma Gandhi who helped liberate the Indian sub-continent. Gandhi once remarked that God is the Supreme Democrat: he gave men free will.

I have often thought that if God had made a senate of political and religious leaders prior to creating the world they would strongly have advised him against being so liberal as to endow mankind with freedom. Clockwork oranges are much more contented and far easier to organize.

Alexander Solzhenitsyn, the Soviet writer who learned all about freedom through an eleven-year stay in a concentration camp, says that Stalin was under the illusion that he alone knew how to lead the people to happiness, how to shove its face into happiness, like a blind puppy's into a bowl of milk – 'There, drink up!'[14] It is also a melancholy fact that in 1942 the great and heroic Winston Churchill, while fighting hard to remove 'the Nazi yoke' from Europe, refused even to contemplate the independence of India. In a regrettably memorable sentence, he said: 'I have not become the King's First Minister to preside at the liquidation of the British Empire.' He was right. He was voted out; and his successor presided.

We all run sovereign empires in miniature whose possible liquidation pains us. A boss enslaves his secretary in the office and in turn is tied by his socialite wife to the non-stop wheel of bridge and cocktail parties. A few adolescents, mouthing liberal slogans, try to impose their will on every-one around. In the home, a big brother plays the part of Big Brother; and a bawling infant gives a pretty good impersonation of a budding Führer.

For all the breathing of the Spirit, how hard it is to be an altogether liberated person. Impossible while remaining a slave to whims and fashions and media-ideologies. Bees in bonnets make an awful lot of buzz because they are not free.

To be free is to be like Christ. That means serving one another indiscriminately, loving our enemies, praying for those who persecute us and – what is sometimes harder – praying for those who persecute the down-trodden and the poor. We are not real disciples of Christ unless we want to free not only the poor from their chains but the exploiters from their crimes. It does not help to love the weak by hating the strong. The perpetrators of racism and apart-heid, of the more vicious forms of communism, capitalism and ecclesiasticism – they are our brothers quite as much as their broken victims. In this at least they are our way-ward brothers, brothers whose actions we must do all in our power to restrain and reverse. But brothers all the same. We have no right to criticize them or try and correct them unless we love them. How else will hatred – the source of every evil – cease? Was it not the absence of love that knocked the Russian Revolution off course and led inexorably to the satanic purges of the Stalinist era? Wasn't the only fault of George Jackson, the Soledad Brother, that he loved selectively just as the white men who ruined his life had done?[15] He alone among us is really free who is like God in having no enemies and loving everyone – the unlovable included. This is the love *for which* Christ's Spirit set us free.

St Augustine is reputed to have said, Love and do what you like. He is not afraid of the consequences because he knows that the loving person only likes to do loving things. Paul, speaking idealistically, says, The law is finished for those who are in Christ Jesus. In Paul's view, it was Christ not Moses who finally and irretrievably smashed the tablets on which the ten commandments were inscribed. When a person is 'in-Spired' by love it is folly to try to regulate his life by telling him, 'Thou shalt not.'

The Christian is very conscious that, having accepted Christ, he does not live from his own resources any more. He regrets that he is not as free as he should be, as free as the wind. Still, he goes on praying, Come, Holy Spirit, hoping that one day the Wind and Freedom of God will take possession of him as it took possession of the apostles at Pentecost. 'Suddenly a sound came from heaven like the rush of a mighty wind, and it filled all the house where they were sitting' (Acts 2:2). Then they were imbued with a mysterious power from on high that lifted them out of their fearful selves to make them the first freedom-marchers of the Christian era. A wind of change swept over the ancient world. And they unlocked the doors of the upper room, flung them wide open and went out like freed men 'to the ends of the earth'.

Discussion questions

In what circumstances do you find the wind annoying? – pleasing? – helpful? – indispensable? Why in the Jewish Bible did the wind seem perfectly suited to be 'God's messenger'? What does Christ mean by the words: 'Do not be surprised that I said to you, "You must be born anew." The wind blows where it wills, and you hear the sound of it, but you do not know whence it comes or whither it goes; so it is with everyone who is born of the Spirit'?

What does freedom mean to most people you know? Can you recall an incident in your life in which you experienced real liberation? Have you ever helped another person to become free?

Is contemporary society freer than the society of yesterday? Is capitalism a freer system than communism? What changes would you like to see brought about so as to ensure greater genuine freedom at school? in the home? in the city? in the country?

Was Pope John wise to open that window? The Church is said to have become more liberal since Vatican II, but has she become more genuinely free?

Can a man be really free when he and his family are starving?

When Jesus said, 'That which is born of flesh is flesh, and that which is born of the Spirit is spirit', did he mean to oppose man's body and his spirit? If not, what is meant by 'flesh' and 'spirit'?

Do you really think that we should love persecutors as much as the persecuted? Is there such a thing as violent love or is love by definition non-violent? Were Gandhi and Martin Luther King really non-violent just because they did not resort to physical force? Has freedom ever been won except by superior force?

Is it gospel-truth or heresy to say that the Spirit has released us from the obligation to keep the ten commandments?

Have you ever met anyone whom you would characterize unreservedly as a free man? Would he have been easy to live with?

4. *Fire*

Spirit of Jesus, Fire of Whitsun,
We so need your light and love.
Send us one parted tongue of your own fire
From above.

THE FASCINATION OF FIRE

'Come and see the blaze, son.' I eagerly leaped out of the primitive underground shelter we had sunk in our garden and held my father's hand. A thousand suns were setting over London. The Nazis had dropped incendiary bombs on the docks and warehouses of the city's East End; and, now that the all-clear had sounded, from our vantage point a few miles away we saw this steady red and orange hue on the horizon. For an eight-year-old it was marvellous and frightening.

Fire is fascinating, I suppose, because it combines in equal degrees beauty and danger; it both appeals and appals. A child is deeply interested, for example, when he approaches a beckoning flame and tries to fix the exact point where pleasure turns to pain. When he comes too close, how stunned he is to find that anything so beautiful should hurt so much. He receives his first bitter lesson in morality.

'Be careful with that match!' Ah, but it was nice to strike a match because, despite the warnings of elders, a match is a domesticated form of fire. Still dangerous, of course, but not too dangerous; and, in any case, its sudden and ephemeral beauty more than compensated for occasional singed hair and eyebrows. Some games are far more dangerous than this. Mankind might be defined as the only animal that plays with fire, even when, in the case of nuclear devices, it threatens to destroy him. There is much truth in the ancient myth in which Prometheus, having made man out of the slime of the earth, animates him with fire filched from heaven.

Fire has many meanings and associations. The nostalgic flavour of 'Keep The Home Fires Burning' would have vanished if its opening line had been 'Keep The Central Heating At A Steady Seventy-Five'. 'Hearth and Home' is so much more comforting than 'Boiler and Home' or even 'Radiator and Home'. Families simply do not sit and chat around boilers and radiators. Leaving aside all value judgements, nothing symbolizes better the change in our way of life than that the focus in most homes has shifted from the flickering fire to the flickering television set.

I remember with feeling the household fire of my earliest years, so warm and comforting, like a glowing heart in the centre of the home. When my grandmother was very old she used to light a fire in her small black grate even in summer. Perhaps she saw in the flames the faces and places of her youth. 'It's so friendly, my dears,' she used to say to us when we entered her house panting and perspiring after a strenuous run. And it *was* friendly just to look upon.

Then there were camp-fires: they denoted fellowship. There were the drifting, smokey fires of autumn in gardens where the leaves had fallen: they were sad affairs, golden rituals of mourning for the end of summer. There were the bonfires of November 5th, Guy Fawkes day: they meant exultation and, in some sense, devilment. There were the bonfires, too, on V.E. Day: they meant that the war was over, no more carnage, only joy, celebration, reunion of loved ones. Fires are like faces, all different though very much alike.

A fire during the day-time was not half so exciting as a fire at night. The night exaggerates everything: hopes, fears, joy, desires, discontent. Imagination, too. This may account for the tradition – stemming perhaps from Homer – that blind story-tellers are the best. In the dark all things are possible and all things can be believed. Night is the time for hatching revolutions, making love, dreaming dreams. In the light of day even stars and quasars disappear. There was something about the flames climbing up the night sky that made the heart soar like a spark. I must confess that even now when I see films of fires – buildings, refineries, racing-cars, the self-combustion of a Buddhist monk – the horror is more than a little tinged with only half-suppressed memories of boyish excitement.

A last recollection: as an adolescent I cycled from the north-west coast of France to Lourdes on the edge of the Pyrenees. What remains clearest in my mind is the journey through the flat forests of the Landes. Pines. Mile after mile of pines. And still more pines. In the early summer evening as the dew began to fall the forest was dank and immobile; seemingly harmless. But countless memorials along the route told another tale. This one honoured the memory of sixty men who had lost their lives putting out a forest fire; the next honoured a hundred brave fire-fighters who had died as hideous a death as Joan of Arc. The catalogue of victims was very long.

When James in his Epistle deals with malicious talk, he likens it to the voraciousness of fire. 'How great a forest is set ablaze by a small fire! And the tongue is a fire. The tongue is an unrighteous world among our members, staining the whole body, setting on fire the cycle of nature, and set on fire by hell' (3:5–6).

ISRAEL'S THEOLOGY OF FIRE

The Israelites had become a people in the desert. Who knows, it may have been around camp-fires at night that their story-tellers began to shape the sagas which eventually found their way into the scriptures. Stories like flames grow taller in the dark.

In the Bible, fire – like water and wind – stands for the presence of God. In Exodus, an angel of the Lord appears to Moses in a flame of fire in the middle of a bush. The bush was burning but not dying. As Moses approached, God called to him from the bush: 'Do not come near; put off your shoes . . . for the place on which you are standing is holy ground' (Exod. 3:5). God identifies himself as 'the God of your father, the God of Abraham, the God of Isaac, and the God of Jacob'. Moses instinctively covers his face, for he is afraid to look at God. Fire usually lives by dying. (It was this essential flux, this contradictoriness of fire that caused the ancient philosopher Heraclitus to choose it as the basic 'substance' underlying everything in this non-sensical world.) But Israel's God is an undying flame of fire.

Later, when the people had escaped from Egypt and gone into the desert, the Lord came down upon Sinai for all to see. 'And Mount Sinai was wrapped in smoke, because the Lord descended upon it in fire; and the smoke of it went up like the smoke of a kiln, and the whole mountain quaked greatly' (Exod. 19:18). Lightning flashes on the mountain-top: a daunting prospect and a superb symbol of the un-approachable holiness of God. It was from the heart of fire that Moses was to receive the commandments designed to fashion a holy people worthy of so holy a God.

When Israel wanted to depict God's presence among them they spoke of the cloud of Yahweh covering the tabernacle by day and fire covering it by night (Exod. 40:38; Numb. 9:16). Yahweh alone is Israel's leader and guide; by following him they need never go astray.

In Israel's theology, Yahweh is fire for a number of reasons. Without him they felt lost in the long and lonely night. Fire which was used to burn away the dross from precious metals also admirably symbolized God's holiness. The meaning of the holocaust, the most solemn sacrifice, however, was not that the victim was destroyed and erased from memory by fire, a fate Hitler intended for Jews when he ordered the public burning of their books. It meant rather that the unblemished victim was hallowed, consumed, transferred into the pure fire-world of God. Human beings are sinners, cold and tainted. This is why they find God's holiness both attractive and repellent, the essence of 'the fascinating'. Simultaneously they want to look and turn away. Another characteristic of fire is that it is alive and without a fixed or final form. In this way, too, it represents the living God whose ways are free and unpredictable. This is probably the real reason why Jews were forbidden to make images of him: he never sits still enough for a satisfactory portrait to be painted of him. Finally, fire is all-consuming; in this it expresses the jealous nature of God who desires the whole heart of his creatures and burns up all rivals in his path: 'I will send fire upon Judah,' says Yahweh, 'and it shall devour the strongholds of Jerusalem' (Amos 2:5).

The prophets' teaching is liberally laced with fire. Jeremiah feels God's word in his heart worse than a wound; it is a kind of 'burning fire shut up in my bones, and I am weary with holding it in, and I cannot' (20:9). The first Isaiah says it needed a burning coal from the temple altar to cleanse his unclean lips. One of the Burning Ones, the Seraphim, 'touched my mouth and said: Behold, this has touched your lips; your guilt is taken away, and your sin forgiven' (6:7). Only then was Isaiah courageous enough to respond to Yahweh's question 'Whom shall I send?' with 'Here I am! Send me!'

The third Isaiah, like the other prophets, looks forward to the Day of the Lord, the Day of Judgement:

> For behold, the Lord will come in fire,
>   and his chariots like the storm-wind,
> to render his anger in fury,
>   and his rebuke with flames of fire.
> For by fire will the Lord execute judgement (66:15–16).

In this apocalyptic vein he goes on to depict the new heaven and the new earth. The faithful of Israel, he says, 'shall go forth and look on the dead bodies of the men that have rebelled against me; for their worm shall not die, their fire shall not be quenched, and they shall be an abhorrence to all flesh' (66:24).

Fire is beautiful; it can also be venomous. It is awesome and, at times, awful. A God who is Fire is someone to be reckoned with.

When Blaise Pascal died in 1662, a crumpled piece of paper was found in his coat. On it was a prayer which began:

Fire.
'God of Abraham, God of Isaac, God of Jacob' (Exod. 3:6), not of philosophers and savants.
Certainty. Certainty. Feeling. Joy. Peace.
God of Jesus Christ.

THE MAN WHO SET THE WORLD ALIGHT

John the Baptist said of Jesus to the crowds: 'He will baptize you with the Holy Spirit and with fire' (Matt. 3:11). The Spirit and the Fire are God himself in his unfathomable holiness. Jesus characterizes his mission with the words: 'I came to set the world on fire and would that it were already kindled' (Luke 12:49).

Like Isaiah before him, Jesus has a vivid, overpowering sense of the holiness of God who alone has the right to be called good (Mark 10:18). 'Whoever says, You fool! shall be liable to the hell of fire' (Matt. 5:22). 'Every tree that does not bear good fruit is cut down and thrown into the fire' (Matt. 7:19). At the close of the age the weeds shall be gathered for burning (Matt. 13:40). Jesus does not flinch from using Isaiah's apocalyptic imagery of unquenchable fire with which to threaten and, yes, *frighten* those who scandalize any of his little ones (Mark 9:42ff). They will be thrown into hell 'where their worm does not die, and the fire is not quenched. For every one will be salted with fire.' Fire, far from destroying them, will be their preservative; they will be pickled with fire. Small wonder that the Apocalypse draws a picture of Christ that we see reflected faithfully in Byzantine art: 'His head and his hair were white as white wool, white as snow; his eyes were like a flame of fire' (Rev. 1:14). This is not the 'gentle Jesus meek and mild' of the little children's hymnal but the all-holy Scrutinizer of the heart, the Judge of living and dead.

But fire does not only burn; it enlightens, warms and consoles.

The first property of fire is light. We tend to forget that formerly the only nightly illumination people had was that given by a naked flame.

Light is the first of God's creatures. When, in the Genesis myth, God creates the world, he first separates light from darkness (1:4). Each morning we see a re-enactment of this wonder: when the sun rises, it is as if God is creating the world anew out of the sable waters of the night.

Jesus said the eye is a lamp inside us: it lights up the whole body which, without it, is only a dark cavern. It is because of the eye that hands, head, arms, legs, feet – the whole body – is able to see its way. A man with eyes is full of light. In the dark, on the contrary, we only stumble and fall and hurt ourselves. A man who goes blind has a foretaste of the darkness of death.

This explains the reader's revulsion at Tanizaki's story, *A Portrait of Shunkin*.[16] Shunkin, a haughty Japanese beauty, is blind. She is one day unaccountably and maliciously injured with the result that she loses her looks. At this, her obsequious lover, Sasuke, makes sure that he will never embarrass her or hurt her pride by gazing at her disfigurement: he makes *himself* blind. He sits down at a mirror and thrusts a sewing needle to the depth of a quarter of an inch into the soft pupil of first his left eye, then the right. It is not merely the pain of this action that appals us but its barbarity. To make oneself blind is deliberately to turn out the light of the world. It is of those who wilfully inflict blindness on themselves that Jesus ironically said: 'For judgement I came into this world . . . that those who see may become blind' (John 9:39).

In John's gospel, Jesus is represented in Exodus terms not only as the Passover lamb and the manna in the wilderness but also as the pillar of fire. This is why Jesus says: 'I am the light of the world; he who follows me will not walk in darkness but will have the light of life' (8:12). The Galilean is the presence of God and he goes before his disciples across the black desert of life lighting up the way. 'As long as I am in the world,' he says, 'I am the light of the world' (9:5). This is symbolized in the Church's ceremony of the Easter Vigil. The risen Christ, represented by the paschal candle, is the solitary source from which comes soon a glow powerful enough to overcome the night.

In the gospel story, Jesus' resurrection is anticipated at the transfiguration when he becomes momentarily a lightning flash, a living torch, upon the mountain-side. But he still had to undergo the great hallowing of death. He still had to be baptized again (Luke 12:50) with the Spirit and with fire. At his resurrection, Jesus was so inflamed by the Spirit he *became* fire and, as he had promised, proceeded to set the world alight.

The Lord is light. In the creed, we confess that the Son is light from light. This light came into the world; only, many preferred darkness to light because their deeds were evil. But the Father of lights who said, Let light shine out of darkness, still shines in our hearts to give the light of the knowledge of the glory of God on the face of Christ (2 Cor. 4:6). The face of the risen Christ is the sun of the new creation.

When Vincent van Gogh, a Dutchman, left his northern home and went to the south of France he was overwhelmed by the dazzling radiance of a sun the like of which he had never seen before. From then onwards, his canvases were invaded by the bright colours that now daily stung his eyes. When he had to go into hospital at Saint-Rémy, he was on occasions confined to his tiny cell. Prevented from wandering abroad into the sun-soaked countryside, he took to copying the prints of the great masters, though modifying them in his own inimitable way. He copied, for example, Jean-François Millet's 'The Sower'. His reproduction, for all its genius, is very close to the original. Then van Gogh set himself the task of painting the 'Raising of Lazarus' on the basis of Rembrandt's etching. He retains Rembrandt's picture-composition except that the tall, commanding, central figure of Christ is missing. In its place, van Gogh has painted in the flaming southern sun.

The man who was born blind (John 9) had been living in a world on which no sun had ever risen. To his blank eyes the Lord gave sight. The first thing he saw was Christ's own face. In the light of Christ he saw light. He was gazing on the Sun.

The 'darkness' from which the blind man – he, you, I – was rescued was godlessness, unbelief. He gained wisdom, an inner light of mind and heart, by which he saw who the man from Nazareth really was: the Christ of God, the eye-opener of God in a world congenitally blind.

The inner light is always the Spirit. Jesus promised those who love him that he will send the Counsellor to be with them for ever, 'even the Spirit of truth, whom the world cannot receive, because it neither sees him nor knows him' (John 14:17). 'The Counsellor, the Holy Spirit, whom the Father will send in my name, he will teach you all things, and bring to your remembrance all that I have said to you' (John 14:26). The Spirit is the teacher within who enlightens us about truth, about Christ.

One more property of fire is warmth. This is why love and affection are often spoken of as 'warm' and why kind people are said to have 'warm personalities'. It was because God sent his Spirit upon Jesus crucified that he was raised up to a new life of love and communion with his Father. The Spirit is therefore the bond of love between Father and Son. Luke intimates what John states expressly (20:22): the Spirit of love was given on Easter day itself. The two disciples who had met Jesus on the road to Emmaus said to each other: 'Did not our hearts *burn within us* while he talked to us on the road, while he opened to us the scriptures?' (24:32)

At Whitsun, God's Seraph hovered over the disciples; the Spirit came in power. 'And there appeared to them tongues as of fire, distributed and resting on each of them' (Acts 2:3). Just as the Spirit came upon Jesus at his baptism and remained with him, so the Spirit came down permanently on his followers at Pentecost. Peter explains to the crowd that Jesus has been raised by God from ignominious death. 'Being therefore exalted at the right hand of God, and having received from the Father the promise of the Holy Spirit, he has poured out this which you see and hear' (Acts 2:33). The Spirit was locked in the disciples' hearts 'as it were a burning fire' in their bones. Like Jeremiah they had no choice but to do what God's Spirit bade them do. They spoke with God's own wisdom and warmth; and the Word spread like a forest fire.

The author of Acts manages to convey through startling imagery that at Whitsun 'the last times' have come; it is the springtime of a new world. Young men's visions and old men's dreams are realized now that God's Spirit has been poured out on all flesh. Wonders in the heavens and prodigies on earth. As Joel wrote, there will be

> Blood and fire and vapour of smoke;
> the sun shall be turned into darkness
> and the moon into blood,
> before the day of the Lord comes,
> the great and manifest Day (2:30–31, Acts 2:20).

Some men believe what they see; others, more fortunate, see what they believe. Only those who see visions and have dreams of what does not yet exist can walk into tomorrow with calmness and joy.

A WHITSUNTIDE WORLD

Whitsun warns us that there is and always has been a raging Fire at the heart of the world. Christ the divine Incendiarist, the man who was burnt up with zeal for his Father's house, said from the beginning that the Spirit had anointed him to preach good news to the poor, to proclaim release for prisoners, to give sight to the blind and freedom to all who are oppressed (Luke 4:18).

While the New Testament is a very religious book, it is not what we might call today a 'churchy' book. This is because the central figure, Jesus Christ, though profoundly religious, was not in any notable sense an ecclesiastic. He was a devout Jewish layman intent on doing God's will in the small but significant area of life in which God had placed him. Like the prophets, he kept his eyes fixed on mercy, justice and truth. 'Go and learn what this means,' he said fiercely to some Pharisees, ' "I desire mercy, and not sacrifice" ' (Matt. 9:13). He proclaimed God's kingly rule in the world, the characteristics of which are poverty, meekness, a hunger and thirst for righteousness, mercy, peace, purity of heart. These things he set above laws, even the most sacred law of Sabbath-keeping. The ecclesiastics of his day found this intolerable. They charged him with heresy and handed him over to the secular arm for crucifixion.

But before he died, Jesus had satisfactorily established the criterion by which his disciples could be known whatever their overt profession of belief or unbelief: not the keeping of laws alone, but the living of the beatitudes.

Whoever rights wrongs, feeds the hungry, cares for the dispossessed not merely with enthusiasm but with dogged determination; whoever is meek and poor and pure of heart; whoever is sensitive towards the numerous little heart-aches people suffer, is – knowingly or unknowingly – an envoy of Christ. And whoever shares in Christ's mission, shares in the Fire of the Spirit.

Nor is it only prophets who have flashes of inspiration. Ordinary people, also, see – sometimes to their surprise and horror – that they are being bigoted towards bigots, unloving towards the unloving, harsh towards the unmerciful. 'I was blind and now I see.'

A parent or teacher who helps youngsters to be sensitive to beauty, enables them to love truth, to honour sincerity, is also a Paraclete, a light and a fire. Theirs is a humbling task. Light and fire can be transmitted but not handled, possessed, understood. They are essentially the personal gift of the Spirit.

Finally, whoever has been warmed by love perceives

however dimly, its eternity. Love is like fire. Love comes from love as fire from fire; and once extinguished it cannot be relit. In this, too, human love is the gift of that Mystery in which all life originates and is grounded.

Whitsun is the feast day of fire, of Fire whipped by divine Wind. Christians celebrate it on behalf of all mankind, for all people are living in a Whitsuntide world. The God of Jesus Christ is the same God who made the heavens and the earth. 'He is,' in the words of *The Upanishads*, 'the one light that gives light to all; he shining, everything shines.'[17] He is in the heart of loving people as a burning fire.

Fire is beautiful, warming, consoling, all-consuming, enlightening, purifying, sanctifying and . . . dangerous. The inspired authors, by representing God's Spirit as fire, guarantee that we will never be tempted to trivialize or try to domesticate the *mysterium tremendum et fascinans*, the tremendous and awesome Mystery in whom we live and move and are.

Discussion questions

Who is the warmest person you know? What kind of effect on others does this person have?

When did you last see a fire of any sort? Which are the fires that have meant most to you in your lifetime? Do you regret in any way the passing of the old coal and wood fires?

What significance do you see in the story of Moses and the burning bush? Is this really a children's story? What connection is there between the Moses story and Pentecost? Do you find it consoling or frightening that God should be represented in scripture as fire? Ought we to be afraid of God?

What did Christ mean when he said, 'I came to set the

world on fire and would that it were already kindled'?
To what extent has his mission been fulfilled? In the
West? In Russia and China? Who carries out Christ's
mission today and how?

Did Christ come primarily to found a Church or to bring
in the kingdom of God? What is the difference? Who
belongs to the kingdom of God?

Analyse the deeper meanings hidden in the story of the man
born blind whom Jesus healed. Have you ever had a
sudden illumination that changed your life radically?

5. *Anointing*

Spirit of Jesus, God's Anointing,
Make us holy, make us strong.
Next to the cross of Christ our Saviour is where
    We belong.

ANOINTED ON THE BEACH

Recently, while lying on a baking Spanish beach, I was drawn to analyse the tomfoolery of sunbathing. One cannot imagine Africans or Arabs doing it. In the days of Jane Austen, western women liked to present a moon-like complexion to the world. Medically, I'm told, it is far from certain that a healthy tan really is healthy after all. But sunbathing is the fashion at present so, bound by the cords of family affection, I laid myself down, dutifully but not uncomplainingly, upon the aforesaid beach. We had paid a lot of money for the trip; it had to be enjoyed.

Apart from second-degree burns I escaped with nothing worse than my life. I owe my survival to the liberal dousings with oils given me in relays by family and friends. In an immediately intelligible sense those oils proved to be my 'health and salvation', though there were hallucinatory moments when I felt I was being anointed for my burial.

ANOINTING IN BIBLICAL TIMES

Olive trees grow everywhere in the Mediterranean area, even in the stoniest ground. The oil from olives has many uses, one of which I now feel confident is as a shield against the sun. In biblical times its range was extended by mixing it with sweet-smelling balsam. Many of its uses have been isolated in recent generations to become major competitive industries, but in the time we're talking about it was employed as sun lotion, ointment and balm for wounds, perfume and deodorant, hair-oil, cooking-oil, rubbing-oil for stiff or strained ligaments, face-cream, lubricant (for inside and out). It also had deep religious significance in the anointing of the dead, the dedication of altars, and the consecration of priests and kings.

A few scattered allusions from the Bible. There never was a juicier, more aromatic picture of brotherhood than the one presented in Psalm 133:

> Behold, how good and pleasant it is
>   when brothers dwell in unity!
> It is like the precious oil upon the head,
>   running down upon the beard,
> upon the beard of Aaron,
>   running down on the collar of his robes (vv. 1–2).

Brotherhood, the Psalmist is saying, is a thing of holiness and joy like the consecration of the High Priest. Incidentally, Aaron's anointing, unlike modern sacramental ceremonies, seems to have been something more than a token gesture.

The Psalmist, in perhaps the most popular prayer in the Jewish Bible, says of Yahweh, the Shepherd of Israel:

> Thou preparest a table before me in the presence of my foes; thou anointest my head with oil, my cup overflows (Ps. 23:5).

Bread, wine and oil were all vital to the enjoyment of a feast. With balsam-perfumed oil the guests' heads were anointed as a sign of the respect and esteem in which they were held by their hosts. This explains Jesus' complaint to Simon the Pharisee who had invited him to a meal and pointedly omitted to do him the customary honours. Simon obviously didn't think highly of Jesus for consorting with

outcasts and sinners and probably only invited him to his
house out of curiosity. It was left to 'a woman of the city
who was a sinner' to bring an alabaster flask of ointment
she had bought in order to honour him. She wet Jesus' feet
with her tears, wiped them with her hair, kissed them
reverently, and finally anointed them with the ointment
(Luke 7). Later in the gospels, when Mary, the sister of
Lazarus, offered Jesus the same courtesy at Bethany, Judas
complained of the waste, saying that the money lavished
on the costly nard would have fed a large number of the
poor. Jesus defended her with the prophetic remark: 'Let
her alone, let her keep it for the day of my burial' (John
12:7).

The Israelites used to consecrate altars and priests
with oil to symbolize God's sweet, abiding presence. The
prophets, though not outwardly anointed, were regarded
as being inwardly anointed by the Spirit of God. It was the
Spirit that charged them to proclaim God's sacred message:

The Spirit of the Lord God is upon me,
  because the Lord has anointed me
to bring good tidings to the afflicted . . .
  to give Zion a garland instead of ashes,
the oil of gladness instead of mourning (Is. 61:1–3).

The kings of Israel were God's chosen ones in a special
sense, hence they were anointed by a priest or prophet – a
ceremony which remains one of the most solemn in the
coronation ritual of the British monarchy. The anointing
of David by Samuel in 1 Samuel 16 is vividly told. Samuel
came to Bethlehem in search of a successor to Saul whom
God had rejected. The Lord told Samuel to fill his horn
with oil and go to Jesse the Bethlehemite, 'for I have pro-
vided for myself a king among his sons'. Samuel was forbidden to choose the tallest or the handsomest, as if these
things mattered in themselves. 'Man looks on the outward

appearance, but the Lord looks on the heart.' Samuel therefore rejected the first seven of Jesse's sons and insisted that the last, the humblest who was keeping the sheep, should be brought before him. It was David:

Now he was ruddy, and had beautiful eyes, and was handsome. And the Lord said, 'Arise, anoint him; for this is he.' Then Samuel took the horn of oil, and anointed him in the midst of his brothers; and the Spirit of the Lord came mightily upon David from that day forward.

Oil was used for these important functions because it was a sign of richness, of gladness, of permanence. Oil was a substance that had to be rubbed into a person; it penetrated the pores. In the days before detergents it was difficult stuff to remove. Anointing with oil in religious ceremonies emphasized that God's Spirit had come down upon his representatives, had penetrated to the core of their personality, and would abide with them for ever if they kept faithful to their office.

The anointing of the king, God's servant or son, in time took on special significance. In Israel's dream of a glorious future, a dream-king often had pride of place. David, whose life had not been free from brutality and emotional entanglements, was idealized: another would come like him, someone dear to God's heart, David's son. The king was sometimes known simply as *mashiah*, the Anointed One, the Messiah. The Jewish liturgy of regal anointing was taken over to dramatize the glory Israel would have 'in the last times'. The Lord and his Anointed (the Messiah) would overcome the world:

I will set my king
  on Zion, my holy hill.
I will tell the decree of the Lord:
  He said to me, 'You are my son,

today I have begotten you.
Ask of me, and I will make the nations your heritage
and the ends of the earth your possession' (Ps. 2:6–8).

It may seem strange that this vision of the kingdom remained long after the disappearance of the monarchy at the time of the Exile in Babylon. But had not God made a solemn promise?

I will not violate my covenant . . .
I will not lie to David.
His line shall endure for ever,
his throne as long as the sun before me.
Like the moon it shall be established for ever;
it shall stand firm while the skies endure (Ps. 89:34–37).

The messianic ideal came to the fore when prophets like the second Isaiah began preaching about universal salvation. One day all men would be converted and worship the one God together. The Messiah, the Son of David, would inaugurate God's kingdom. Despite all the fantastic imagery with which it was described, it was to be a kingdom of peace, plenty and righteousness. Israel, through all the sadness of the years, never lost her intense belief in the perfectibility of men. In the kingdom that was coming, God would reign through his righteous One. Jeremiah spoke of Yahweh as 'the Lord our righteousness' (23:6). Through the Messiah, God would bring into being a new order of justice and gentleness:

The sucking child shall play over the hole of the asp,
and the weaned child shall put his hand on the adder's den.
They shall not hurt . . . in all my holy mountain;
for the earth shall be full of the knowledge of the Lord
as the waters cover the sea (Is. 11:8–9).

Isaiah's successor stressed that this ideal of peace was

impossible without affliction. He proposes the figure of the Servant of God which is Israel:

Behold my Servant, whom I uphold,
  my chosen in whom my soul delights;
I have put my Spirit upon him,
  he will bring forth justice to the nations.
He will not cry or lift up his voice,
  or make it heard in the street;
a bruised reed he will not break,
  and a dimly burning wick he will not quench (Is. 42:1–2).

God's Servant will be a Suffering Servant:

He was despised and rejected by men;
  a man of sorrows, and acquainted with grief . . .
Surely he has borne our griefs
  and carried our sorrows;
yet we esteemed him stricken,
  smitten by God, and afflicted (Is. 53:3–4).

Israel was conscious even then of being the world's scapegoat, of having to suffer on behalf of all mankind. But she was conscious as well that she also had sinned. If, therefore, the Suffering Servant, at one level, was the people of Israel, at another level it stood for their own representative who would atone for Israel's sins too. Though this Servant pour out his soul in death and be numbered among the transgressors (Is. 53:12), yet it is on him that God's anointing Spirit rests. It is because of him that many shall one day be accounted righteous. There was to be no rose-strewn path to Messiahship and the kingdom of God.

THE ANOINTED ONE OF GOD

Jesus became Lord and Christ (the Anointed of God) by his death and resurrection. The Spirit of God which over-

shadowed Mary when Jesus was conceived now descends
upon the Crucified to make him Lord and Christ. Jesus
'who was descended from David according to the flesh [was]
constituted Son of God in power according to the Spirit of
holiness by his resurrection from the dead, Jesus Christ our
Lord' (Rom. 1:3–4).

It is a mistake to think that Jesus accepted messianic
titles for himself. He seems to have ignored if not rejected
the acclaim of the people to be the Son of David or Son of
God. From the beginning of his ministry he resolutely
adopted the stance of the Servant of God. He humbly
referred to himself as 'son of man', a Hebraism for 'man'
or 'Adam'. Nor was Jesus a priest in any formal or official
sense. He was not a member of the tribe of Levi nor did he
receive the priestly oil of consecration. The Epistle to the
Hebrews speaks of Jesus, a Jewish layman, as our High
Priest figuratively in the sense that he was completely loyal
in his service of God and offered God the sacrifice of his life.

For all this, the evangelists do not hesitate to honour
Jesus as the Christ of God, the Messiah. This is why they
describe Jesus' baptism as his anointing with the Spirit; it
is in the strength of that anointing that he is able to face up
to the Tempter in the desert and can fearlessly carry out
his mission of preaching forgiveness to everyone who
repents. And he applies to himself Isaiah's words: 'The
Spirit of the Lord is upon me, because he has anointed me
to preach good news to the poor' (Luke 4:18).

The Spirit, God's Anointing, never left Jesus; and if he
refused the titles pertaining to the Christ (or Messiah) it was
because he wanted to leave no doubts about the nature of
his mission. The Christ was not about to bring in an era of
easy terrestrial bliss as many of his contemporaries, his
disciples included, supposed. Jesus was going to return to
the highest traditions of the prophets. His task was to
enable his fellow men to enter into a new relationship with

God as Father, even though to do this he must become
Isaiah's Suffering Servant. The kingdom was not to be
characterized by conquest or vainglory but by meekness,
mercy, poverty, purity of heart. Jesus proved he was worthy
to be the Christ by manifesting in himself – especially in his
ministry and his death – all the demands of the kingdom.
His disciples did not grasp this until he had died. When he
was crucified they ran away thinking he was accursed by
God himself. 'Cursed be everyone who hangs on a tree.'
But in a little while they were able to proclaim that he was
by his death the Lord and the Christ. For Jesus crucified had
been raised by God through the power of the Holy Spirit.
His death was not after all a desecration but a consecration.
Even on the cross, his body was anointed by the healing
and sanctifying Spirit. The author of Hebrews, referring to
Christ's death and resurrection, writes:

> Thou hast loved righteousness and hated lawlessness;
> therefore God, thy God, has anointed thee
> with the oil of gladness beyond thy comrades (1:9).

In many ways, of course, the Roman soldiers who tormented Christ were right: he *was* a burlesque king. The
purple cloak, the reed for a sceptre, the crown of thorns,
the high wooden throne – these were in keeping with his
life. 'Jesus of Nazareth King of the Jews.' Many a true
word is spoken in jest.

THE MANY WHO ARE ANOINTED

'Christians' are so called because they are the anointed
followers of the Anointed One. Each of them is called to be
another Christ, to share in his role of Suffering Servant.

At the beginning of discipleship there is an initial
'Christing' or 'Christening' process: baptism, confirmation,
eucharist.

'By one Spirit,' wrote Paul, 'we were all baptized into one body . . . and all were made to drink of one Spirit' (1 Cor. 12:13). In baptism the disciple is sacramentally buried with Christ in death so as to rise with him to a newness of life. From the beginning, therefore, he is sealed by the Spirit (2 Cor. 1:21) and consecrated for the worship of God. Scripture warns him not to 'grieve the Holy Spirit' by which he was sealed for the day of redemption (Eph. 4:30).

In confirmation, the disciple is anointed with oil in the form of a cross. The Christ-life is strengthened or confirmed in him so that through the anointing of the Spirit he may become a prophet of the Lord, ready to spread abroad the message of divine forgiveness. This forgiveness was fully expressed in Christ's love for sinners which was consummated (John 19:30) on the cross.

In the eucharist, the disciple is fully initiated into Christ: he becomes one with him through the prophetic sign of eating Christ's body and drinking his blood. In this way too the Christian life is shown to be the way of the cross since here the believer is joining Christ in his sufferings so as to be worthy to share the resurrection in which they are fulfilled.

The cross is the centre and so the chief symbol of the Christian faith. The sacraments do no more than initiate us into a life that has to develop and deepen each day, with each new experience. Most times, we only *talk about* the cross. Léon Bloy who understood these things wrote: 'Man has places in his heart which do not yet exist, and into them enters suffering in order that they may have existence.'[18] We must become sharers in the sufferings of Christ; there is no other way to rescue the world from hatred and despair. As Aeschylus wrote five centuries before Christ, 'Only those who suffer learn.' And perhaps even more memorably: 'Truth is only learned by suffering it.'

The Holy Spirit is the Spirit of truth (John 16:13). Hopefully, this truth has been rubbed into our inmost being like oil. 'The anointing which you received from [the Son] abides in you, and you have no need that any one should teach you; as his anointing teaches you about everything' (1 John 2:27).

The Spirit's influence may be felt when we least expect it, when God seems furthest away from us. Then we will have the chance to suffer, knowingly and willingly, with the Suffering Servant of God. We may be tempted to think at that moment that Jesus got the recipe for happiness all wrong. With one of Malamud's characters in *The Magic Barrel*, Manischevitz the Jew, we will want to ask: 'Who, after all, was Manischevitz that he had been given so much to suffer? A tailor. Certainly not a man of talent. Upon him suffering was largely wasted. It went nowhere, into nothing; into more suffering.'[19] We will have the impression like Manischevitz that however much we speak to God, God has 'absented himself'. Jesus the Jew felt like that. 'Why so much suffering? Why me, a carpenter?' There are times when God won't talk to you. This is crucifixion. This is the truth Jesus learned by suffering it. And when he learned it he became Christ.

There must be many Christs who have never been baptized or confirmed or shared in any eucharist. Whoever triumphs over pain, failure, humiliation, is anointed with the Spirit and becomes the Christ of God. Whenever anyone makes a stand on behalf of a colleague who has been sacked unjustly and, in so doing, risks being sacked himself, he is Christ. When someone brings joy into a clouded situation, he is Christ. When a woman forgives someone who has offended her, when, as in Dostoevsky's classic case, she even forgives her child's assailant and murderer, she is a martyr or witness of the Spirit of love; she is Christ.

Christ is present as victim as well as hero. When a couple lose their son in a battle far away, Christ suffers in them. The Greeks had a proverb: 'The spring is taken from the year when young men die in war.' The Spirit of Christ is the Healer whom we sometimes mistake for Time. But Time could only 'heal' by making us forget; whereas the Spirit heals by allowing us to hold on to all our memories. And even to hearts which seem to have surrendered spring, he can bring something of the warmth and brightness of summer.

There is only one Christ as there is only one God. He is the anointed One who suffers in everyone. Léon Bloy again:

> Christ is at the centre of things, he takes all things upon himself, he bears all things, he suffers all things. It is impossible to strike a human being without striking him, to humiliate someone without cursing or killing him. The lowest of contemptible fellows is forced to borrow the Face of Christ in order to receive the blow, from no matter what hand. Otherwise the buffet could never reach him and would remain hanging in interstellar space, through the ages of ages, until it should have met with the Face which forgives.[20]

In all our lives there are times when the whole world goes black (Matt. 27:45); and then to our astonishment, a new dawn breaks (Matt. 28:1). Christians speak at such moments of the death and resurrection of Christ. Someone might ask, very puzzled, How can Christ's life and death affect everyone? To such a question, Paul would have responded, even more puzzled, Do you think that anyone can do anything without affecting everyone? Are we not one body? If the hand is hurt, isn't the whole of us hurt; and if the eyes smile, isn't the whole of us happy? Is not each of us Adam, mankind in miniature? Why should you be surprised that Jesus, God's Anointed, is the Christ in all men?

All people are consecrated by love and suffering. The Christian sometimes feels that no longer is he suffering with Christ but Christ is suffering in him. Such moments bring a joy that presages the inexpressible joy of the world to come, a joy that no one can take from us (John 16:22).

Discussion questions

How many TV commercials have you seen recently advertising products which involve some form of 'anointing'?

If some were to say of a friend or acquaintance, 'He's a real Christ-figure', what would you understand him to mean? Should we want Christ-figures, or should we be satisfied with Jesus?

What does it mean to say that Jesus became Christ by his death and resurrection?

Analyse the story in the gospels which appeals to you most dealing with an instance when Jesus was anointed.

Do you think that Christ can have an influence on all men, especially since he died two thousand years ago and never went through the kind of experiences we have to undergo? How can Christ still suffer; and suffer when anyone suffers?

Can you remember an instance when belief in Christ really made you happy?

6. Consoler

Spirit of Jesus, our Consoler,
Take away our hearts of stone.
Give us a peace surpassing everything
The world has known.

A NEW HEART

My favourite tale by Hans Christian Andersen is one of the least known: 'The Teapot.'[21] There was once upon a time a proud porcelain teapot whose only flaw was she had a cracked lid which had been riveted. Despite this, in her own eyes, she was the queen of the tea-table. But one day she was dropped. The spout and the handle joined the lid on the casualty list. The following day she was given away to a beggar woman.

The teapot was destitute and speechless both inside and out. But then 'a better life began'; there was a complete transformation. Dirt was put inside her. For a teapot, that was like being buried. But a flower bulb was put in the dirt. 'And,' the story continues, 'the bulb lay in the dirt, the bulb lay inside me. It became my heart, my living heart. I had never had one like that before. There was life in me, there was vigour and vitality; the pulse beat, the bulb sprouted. It was bursting with thoughts and emotions. It blossomed. I saw it, I bore it, I forgot myself in its loveliness.' Later someone said the plant deserved a better pot. 'I was broken in two. It hurt terribly but the flower was put in a better pot – and I was thrown out in the yard, to lie there like an old fragment. But I have a memory that I cannot lose.'

'Heart-transplant' surgery has caused a great stir in our

day out of all proportion to its medical importance, the reason being that for centuries the heart has been the emblem of love. Witness the often crude but nearly always tender representations of the Sacred Heart or, come to that, the Valentine's day greetings cards.

For the Jews, the heart was more than the source and symbol of affection. They thought of it more broadly as the real self or *spirit*, as what a person 'deep down' is really like. How he thinks, how he feels, how he speaks, how he acts, how he looks on life – all this was covered by the term 'a man's heart'. It is with his whole heart and soul and might that he must seek and serve God (Deut. 4:29). If he sins:

> The sacrifice acceptable to God is a broken spirit;
> a broken and contrite heart, O God, thou wilt not despise
> (Ps. 51:17).

It is clear from this that in scripture a broken-hearted person is not someone who is upset but someone who has repented. A heartless person is not merely someone cruel or unfeeling but someone spiritually destitute, without any affinity to God and spiritual things. It is a calamity for anyone to be hard of heart but equally so to be *blind* of heart; it is profitless to be generous in almsgiving if one lacks interior wisdom and discernment.

We saw how at the time of the Exile the prophets promised Israel that one day a new era would be ushered in. 'They shall be my people, and I will be their God. I will give them one heart and one way, that they may fear me for ever, for their own good and the good of their children after them' (Jer. 32:39). The good exiles were for Jeremiah like sound figs in a mixed basket. The bad figs were too bad to be eaten but as for the good: 'I will give them a heart to know that I am the Lord; and they shall be my people and I will be their God, for they shall return to me with their whole heart' (24:7). Ezekiel speaks in similar terms:

'Cast away from you all the transgressions which you have
committed against me, and get yourselves a new heart and
a new spirit!' (18:31) Then most vividly of all: 'A new heart
I will give you, and a new spirit I will put within you; and
I will take out of your flesh the heart of stone and give you
a heart of flesh' (36:26). The celestial Surgeon promises to
give Israel not a new lease of life but a new life. A 'heart of
flesh' will think and feel and hope and love in ways impossible to an impenetrable 'heart of stone'.

Jeremiah is not afraid to attribute to God himself a heart
of flesh. He who loves Israel faithfully 'with an everlasting
love' (31:3) says:

> Is Ephraim my dear son?
>   Is he my darling child?
> For as often as I speak against him,
>   I do remember him still.
> Therefore my heart yearns for him;
>   I will surely have mercy on him (31:20).

THE CONSOLER HAS COME

When Christ came he was no vain, swashbuckling hero but
'meek and humble of heart' (Matt. 11:29), that is, in
Ezekiel's terms, someone with a heart of flesh. He has the
profound gift of reading 'the thoughts of the heart' (Luke
9:47). He is grieved at his accusers' hardness of heart
(Mark 3:5). He attacks the hypocrites out of whose heart
'come evil thoughts, murder, adultery, fornication, theft,
false witness, slander' (Matt. 15:19). Every one, he warns,
will be called to account for every careless word at Judgement Day, for a word is but the overflow from the heart
(Matt. 12:34). He repeats the first Jewish commandment
to love God with all one's heart. He puts his disciples on
their guard against the dire consequences of not forgiving

their brothers from the heart (Matt. 18:35). He promises the kingdom to those who are 'pure of heart'. Above all, he preaches a God who has a father's heart towards his often wayward children. Paul was taking his cue from Christ when he wrote to the church at Corinth: 'Blessed be the God and Father of our Lord Jesus Christ, the Father of mercies and the God of all consolation who comforts us in all our tribulation' (2 Cor. 1:3–4).

We noted how in the fourth gospel Jesus makes the startling proclamation on the last great day of the Feast of Tabernacles: ' "If any one thirst, let him come to me; and let him drink who believes in me. Out of his [Christ's] heart shall flow rivers of living water." Now this he said about the Spirit which those who believed in him were to receive; for as yet the Spirit had not been given, because Jesus was not yet glorified' (7:39). Christ has within him the new heart of the world. That heart had to be opened (John 19:34) for the Spirit to be poured into the hearts of men.

At the time, Jesus' death seemed to the disciples to be the end of everything. Their messianic hopes had died with him. Messiahs do not get themselves crucified.

John, however, believes that Jesus at the Supper was making them a promise: 'It is better for you I should go away, for if I do not go away the Paraclete will not come to you, but if I go, I will send him to you' (16:7). The Paraclete is both Consoler and Counsellor.

The Consoler will comfort them in 'the little while' of their bereavement. This little while will be remembered no longer than a woman remembers the pangs of childbirth once she experiences the joy of bringing a child into the world. It is true that birth seems like death. That is what Hans Christian Andersen tried to convey in his tale of the teapot: humiliation and terrible hurt can be, for the brave, the way to a new heart and a new life.

The disciples are not to be misled by his humiliating

death by which Jesus, in reality, was born again. He promises to send them the Consoler who will come and wipe away all the tears from their eyes. Nowhere in the scriptures is the divineness and loving personality of the Spirit better expressed than here. If Jesus is God with a Face, the Spirit is here shown to be God with a heart, a heart of flesh.

Since the Spirit is also the Counsellor, he will remove all blindness from the disciples' hearts. He is the Spirit of truth who will lead them into all truth by the light of Christ. 'Whatever he hears,' Jesus says, 'he will speak, and he will declare to you the things that are coming' (16:13). The things that were coming were of supreme importance, namely, his own death and resurrection.

Nothing could be clearer than that Jesus is going away in order to come closer to his disciples than before. He comes in the coming of his Spirit whom he sends from the Father.

THE PEACE OF THE DOVE

The Spirit is the Dove of God. He is the emissary of divine peace. At the Supper, the gift of the Spirit was pledged by Jesus with the words: 'Peace I leave with you; my peace I give to you; not as the world gives do I give to you' (John 14:27).

In John's gospel, the 'world' is not the place we live in but the unholy system that men have constructed for themselves when they do wrong. It is the system of 'darkness' that stands opposed to Christ's kingdom of light. 'The world' can offer peace of a sort but on its own terms. It can offer the soft and easy option, the quiet life that suits people who have allowed their consciences to be blunted. It can appeal to the wilful blindness that obviates the need to research into the deeper and harder things of faith, hope and charity. Christ's peace is perfectly compatible with 'weeping and lamentation', with rejection, persecution, death on a cross. Pain like pleasure comes and goes but peace remains. This is the peace of the Dove, the divine peace conferred by the risen Christ upon his disciples (John 20:21, 26). This is the peace which passes all understanding (Phil. 4:7), proving that its source is the unfathomable Spirit who alone knows the mind and heart of God.

The essence of this peace is that we are forgiven by God on account of Christ who is 'our peace' (Eph. 2:14). To possess it we first have to admit that we have done wrong and need forgiveness. The first great preachers of Christ crucified were Peter and Paul, two repentant sinners. In confessing their sins, they had come to understand the fatherly heart of God. This is why they spoke with an authority which their enemies could not crush. This is why they became peacemakers and were worthy to be called 'children of God'.

Christ's whole ministry was one of forgiveness and reconciliation: 'The son of man came to seek and save the lost' (Luke 19:10). He was the new Jonah, the Dove of God, who cried, 'Repent for the kingdom of God is at hand.' The condition of being forgiven is to forgive. 'How often must I forgive,' asked Peter in an outburst of generosity, 'seven times?' 'No,' said Jesus, 'seventy times seven times,' that is, times without number. Only in this way could his disciples begin to imitate the endlessly forgiving God. Jesus proved he was like his Father when he told Peter to feed his flock even though Peter had denied him three times (John 21).

There is a remarkable story by Isaac Babel, a Jew who ended his days in a Soviet concentration camp, called 'The Sin of Jesus'. The chief character, Arina, had a job as a hotel maid. Many a time she prayed to Jesus complaining about her wretched lot, particularly about the way she was abused by the hotel guests who took her to bed with them whenever they pleased. They seemed to Arina to spit into her soul. 'Was it me,' she complained to Jesus, 'who made my body heavy, was it me that brewed vodka on earth, was it me that created a woman's soul stupid and lonely?' Jesus blushed at her complaints.

The last time Arina was confined, she felt at the end of her tether. She went out into the backyard and raised her swollen belly to the skies:

'What sense there's in it,' [she cried] 'I just can't see. But I've had enough.'

With his tears Jesus laved Arina when he heard these words. The Saviour fell on his knees before her.

'Forgive me, little Arina. Forgive your sinful God for all he has done to you . . .'

But Arina shook her head and would not listen.

'There's no forgiveness for you, Jesus Christ,' she said. 'No forgiveness, and never will be.'[22]

This story, for all its surface blasphemy, has about it a deep and easily recognizable folk-wisdom. Jesus must have been well aware of the crucifying demands he was having to make of his followers if they were to become perfect as his heavenly Father is perfect (Matt. 5:48) and merciful as the Father is merciful (Luke 6:36). Perhaps on his cross he kept begging not only that the Father should forgive us but also that we should forgive him. Sanctity as well as sinfulness needs pardon of a sort, a pardon we are sometimes more than reluctant to grant. In this context, a brilliant remark attributed to Sigmund Freud springs to mind: 'It is easy to understand why Christians throughout the ages have persecuted the Jews. They have never forgiven the Jews for giving them Jesus Christ.'

As Jesus hangs on his cross he does not look like our peace. The way of the cross he tells us to tread does not look like the way of peace. But it is, because it is the only way to forgiveness.

Only after the crucifixion was the forgiving Christ able to breathe on his disciples and say to them, 'Receive the Holy Spirit. If you forgive the sins of any they are forgiven' (John 20:22–23). He gave them the Spirit of the Dove so that they could become doves in their turn and be emissaries of his pardon and peace.

There is no need to state at any length what is now so obvious. Whoever radiates peace, whoever comforts the afflicted and bereaved, is Christ's disciple. Whoever is merciful is blessed. Whoever forgives proves that he, like Christ, has a heart of flesh and has known tribulation.

Towards the end of Tolstoy's masterly *Anna Karenin*, Anna tells Levin to remind his wife, Kitty, that she has lost none of her former affection for her. Kitty has refused to see her on account of her scandalous affair with Count Vronsky. Anna reaches the heights of magnanimity when she adds: 'If she cannot forgive me my position, then I hope she may never forgive me; for to forgive, she would have to go through what I have gone through, and may God spare her that!'[23]

Every forgiving person is dwelt in by the Spirit of Christ crucified. The Spirit has no finer and no more comforting title than that bestowed on him in the liturgy: 'The Forgiveness of Sins'.

Discussion questions

Have you ever had an experience like the one described in Hans Christian Andersen's story of 'The Teapot'?

What do you mean when you speak of someone as being 'good hearted'? What did the Jewish Bible mean by a man's 'heart'? Does this correspond with our usage?

Why do you think that heart-transplant surgery has aroused such interest and controversy in our time?

Have you ever felt very much in need of the consolations of the Spirit? How did these consolations come to you?

What kind of peace does Christ offer us? Dare you relate a moment when you have experienced such peace?

Do you find forgiveness easy? Is it true that one has to suffer in order to learn how to forgive? Is there any person who has wronged you whom you find it hard or even impossible to forgive?

What truth is there in Isaac Babel's story of the Saviour falling on his knees and pleading for forgiveness?

Why did Jesus say to his disciples, 'It is better for you I should go away'? How can life be better for us at Jesus' departure from the world?

7. *First Fruits*

Spirit of Jesus, First fruits in us
Of the Glory God will give,
One day on our dry bones your Breath will come
  And they shall live.

FIRST FRUITS OF THE LAND

Since we mostly live in urban sprawls, we miss the fascination, mystery and wonder of the land.

Come, my beloved,
  let us go forth into the fields,
  and lodge in the villages;
let us go out early to the vineyards,
  and see whether the vines have budded,
whether the grape blossoms have opened
  and the pomegranates are in bloom . . .
The mandrakes give forth fragrance,
  and over our doors are all choice fruits,
new as well as old (Cant. 7:11–13).

The fruits, the golden harvest, ripe apples, lemons, oranges, clusters of burnished dates – for the Jews, these were like so many smiles of God on the earth's face. They told of his bounty. Men plough and sow, water and weed. But God alone is the Lord of every harvest; it is he who gives the increase.

The Israelites were one of many peoples who developed the custom of offering back to God the first fruits of their land. They felt it to be their solemn duty: 'The first of the first fruits of your ground you shall bring into the house of the Lord' (Exod. 23:19). The rituals to be observed were laid down in detail. When harvest came, they were to take a basket of the first fruits to the temple and say to the priest there: 'I declare this day to the Lord your God that I have come into the land which the Lord swore to our fathers to give us' (Deut. 26:3).

Israel had begun her career under Abraham as a nomadic people, and their father, Jacob, had been 'a wandering Aramean'. But a people without a land is like a child without a mother. The Israelites longed for stability in a country of their own and, according to their traditions, God in his saving kindness had given them Canaan, a place to settle in, a land flowing with milk and honey. 'And behold, now I bring the first of the fruit of the ground, which thou, O Lord, hast given me' (Deut. 26:10).

The Israelites had, then, a special reason for their first fruit offerings of early barley at the beginning of Passover week and of ripe wheat on the day of Pentecost: they were returning to God the fruit of the land which he had given them, the fruit of the land of promise.

When I was a child we always considered that the first fruits and vegetables of the season were the best. We always spoke in those days of 'new potatoes' and 'new carrots' as though a fresh world had begun. They certainly were the sweetest and the tenderest, and, as is to be expected, the most expensive.

The Israelites offered the first fruits not simply because they were the choicest but because they had a special significance. Through the first fruits, they considered, the whole harvest was made holy; the part sanctified the whole. St Paul was speaking strictly within his Jewish tradition when he refers to Christ as 'the first fruits of those who have fallen asleep' (1 Cor. 15:20, 23). Christ was the first to rise from the dead; he was the first fruits to spring up out of the dark earth. In Paul's view, Christ is thereby the representative of all people who are destined to conquer death. In fact, he is the guarantee that the rest of the harvest will also rise. Further, the whole harvest is bound to be in some sense holy because Christ, the first fruits, was found holy and acceptable to God.

Christ was raised by the Spirit. It is by the Spirit that he lives in us. This is why Paul declares that we possess 'the first fruits of the Spirit' (Rom. 8:23) within us. Canaan, the land of promise, was itself a sign of the holier and happier Promised Land that awaits us when, at the end of our journey, we receive the redemption of our bodies. It is of this heavenly land that we received the first fruits at Pentecost. The Spirit is the foretaste of heaven; we actually savour now 'the things that are coming'. This is why Paul outlines the fruit of the Spirit as 'love, joy, peace, patience, kindness, goodness, faithfulness, gentleness, self-control' (Gal. 5:22–23). The Christian life should show something of the joy and exultation of a harvest festival.

The Spirit, like Christ, is also the pledge, the guarantee of future happiness. In giving us the Spirit, the Father has given us the first instalment of heaven; and since he is faithful to his promises, full payment will be made when the world's time is ripe.

FIRST FRUITS OF THE GLORY

For the Jews, 'glory' meant the real value of a thing, not what it is in the esteem of men. God's Glory is God himself as revealed in his majesty, holiness and power. This Glory, in Israel's sagas, is perceived in fire, cloud and storm; it fills the temple as a token of his presence (1 Kings 8:10). Whenever God's people believed that God had saved them from some calamity or given them his blessing they reckoned they had seen his Glory.

The New Testament belief is that in the life, death and resurrection of Jesus, God's Glory is finally revealed. Christ is 'the radiance of the Father's Glory'. He is the light of a new creation, for 'it is the God who said, "Let light shine out of darkness", who has shone in our hearts to give the light of the knowledge of the Glory of God in the face of Christ' (2 Cor. 4:6). John's gospel insists astonishingly that Christ was fully and finally transfigured with the Glory of God when he was nailed to the cross on Calvary. It was only when he came to his 'hour' that he was able to pass over to his Father and so become in Paul's term 'the Lord of Glory' (1 Cor. 2:8).

Since the Lord of Glory is already in us by his Spirit, we possess 'eternal life'. This is the life of life; the life within and beyond life; the life that death cannot touch. This is why we can glorify God 'through Jesus Christ' even when we suffer and die (John 21:18). Jesus revealed God's Glory on the cross; so can we through his Spirit who dwells in us. We, like Christ, do not and cannot add to God's Glory but simply manifest it. When we glorify God, we are glorified by him. His Glory shines in us and through us like fire.

Time is overturned because we have within us Christ, the first fruits of the Spirit; we are already tasting the glory to come. 'And we all beholding the Glory of the Lord, are being changed into his likeness from one degree of glory to another; for this comes from the Lord who is the Spirit' (2 Cor. 3:18).

Christ in us 'the hope of Glory' (Col. 1:27). This hope is Christian hope, that is, not wishful thinking but a *certain* promise. All the same, we have to wait patiently for the Glory to be finally revealed in us. Until then there is a painful growing process to be gone through. 'We know,' writes Paul in a poetic passage, 'that the whole creation has been groaning in travail together until now' (Rom

8:22). The whole earth is a mother writhing in labour until God's children see the light of perfect day.

THE BREATH OF LIFE

There must be many mothers whose first sight of their baby convinced them he was still-born. It often takes a smart slap on the back for the child to be able to take his first gulping breath and utter his first cry. Smiles of contentment all round. He's alive after all.

How often a mother creeps by day or night into her child's bedroom, at the risk of waking him, and all to make sure that her little one is *still* breathing. She has heard so many stories . . . The words of the great dancer Nijinsky are true: 'Mothers feel the nearness of death, giving birth to a child.'

It is strange that life and all its wonders should depend on something so fragile and evanescent as the breath in our bodies. While we breathe, we live. For the most part, we are not aware we are breathing. And yet breathing is usually the best pointer to our condition. If we are 'short of breath' it means we are smoking too much or eating too much or simply, alas, ageing too much. We puff and pant and wheeze and sneeze and whistle and sniffle and blow and sigh and yawn. How we breathe depends on whether we are angry, elated, surprised, afraid, sad, exhausted, filled with sexual desire. Anyone who has worked in radio knows that each person has his own breathing pattern which is almost as characteristic as a speech pattern. The editing (or doctoring) of tapes requires a skilled operator who ensures that not a single breath is misplaced. If it is, it is immediately detectable.

How often is death described in terms such as 'he expired' or 'he breathed his last'. Relatives watch over the beds of those they love until they are certain that the last faint sign of life has vanished: they breathe no more. Only then is the long vigil ended.

Between the first painful swallow of air to the last stertorous breath there runs the passage of our life. Our lives are our own and not our own. We are flesh of the flesh of mankind; there is even a time within the womb when someone else breathes for us. But afterwards we breathe for ourselves until the bellows cease and we dissolve into our component dust.

> The books, the wisdom, the long embrace, the kiss,
> Ah, what do they all signify but this:
> After the dark communion comes the pain
> Of leaving the quietness where you have lain;
> The sudden agony of lonely breath,
> The lonely journey and the lonelier death.[24]

The God of the Bible is the giver of life and breath. In the Genesis myth, Yahweh 'formed man from the ground, and breathed into his nostrils the breath of life; and man became a living being' (2:7). Man lives because God has given him the kiss of life. There is a rich ambiguity here: man lives by the breath of God and yet his breath is his own. Further, man begins to live by means of the divine Breath, the Spirit, whereby God himself lives. Man's life originates in the depths of God; it is therefore holy. Dust man may be but there is something of inexpressible value within him all the same: the Breath of the creator. Man, as the Hindu scripture says, does not live by breath alone – but by God the giver of breath.

Job says of God:

> In his hand is the life of every living thing
>   and the breath of all mankind (12:10).

Job swears his lips will not speak falsehood,

> As long as my breath is in me
>   and the Spirit of God is in my nostrils (27:3).

But while Job is certain that 'God's Spirit made me and the breath of the Almighty gave me life' (33:4), what happens to a man when he has breathed his last?

> If he should take back his Spirit to himself
>   and gather to himself his breath,
> all flesh would perish together,
>   and man would return to the dust (34:14).

Is man, then, in spite of God's breath that gives him life, to end up as a heap of dust? Is death a completely breath-taking experience? And afterwards is man nothing more than the dust and ashes of which he is compounded? It seemed so. Even Job was not able to visualize a happiness or hope beyond this life. When death comes, there is only Sheol, the deep dark pit wherein the dead dwell; there, existence is so shadowy, so lonely, so amorphous, that it cannot be characterized as life at all.

This accounts for the scepticism, the world-weariness of the Book of Ecclesiastes. The author, Qoheleth (the Preacher), sees that everywhere under the sun wickedness is in the place of righteousness; the whole earth is topsy-turvy. It is not true, he asserts in splendid defiance of all Israel's traditions, that God always rewards good and punishes evil *in this world*. And since beyond the grave there is nothing but Sheol, there is no hope for any man except to enjoy life while it is there and to thank God for it.

The injustices of the world are part of God's test to show men that they, for all their pretensions, are no different from the beasts:

> For the fate of the sons of men and the fate of beasts is the same; as one dies, so dies the other. They all have the same breath, and man has no advantage over the

beasts; for all is vanity. All go to one place; all are from the dust, and all turn to dust again. Who knows whether the spirit of man goes upward and the spirit of the beast goes down to the earth? (3:19–21)

The cynicism of Qoheleth seems perilously close to that of Omar Khayyám:

> And if the Wine you drink, the Lip you press,
> End in the Nothing all Things end in – Yes –
>   Then fancy while Thou art, Thou art but what
> Thou shalt be – Nothing – Thou shalt not be less.

AFTER THE LAST BREATH?

In spite of his cynicism, Qoheleth performed an invaluable service to religion. He refused to deny the evidence of his senses: earthly sanctions on good and evil are in no way adequate. The best people can and do live and die in agony, while the evil pass their days rich and tranquil. He squarely and fearlessly laid the responsibility for this on God the creator. Injustice is as much part of the world God made as sunlight and rain. It was this severe questioning of God which eventually led Israel to believe in an after-life. How else could we be sure that God is true to himself and acts honourably towards good people who love him?

Israel's depiction of the after-life was strongly dependent on an image found in the prophet Ezekiel (chapter 37).

Ezekiel saw in a vision a valley full of bones which were very dry. The Lord said to him: 'Son of man . . . prophesy to these bones, and say to them, O dry bones, hear the word of the Lord. Thus says the Lord God to these bones: Behold I will cause breath to enter you, and you shall live. And I will lay sinews upon you, and will cause flesh to come upon you, and cover you with skin, and put breath in you, and

you shall live; and you shall know that I am the Lord'
(37:3–6).

The winds blew; there was a rattling, and bone was
joined to bone. Then sinews and flesh covered the bones;
but still there was no breath in them until Ezekiel in
obedience to God commanded the four winds to breathe
upon the slain. And when the breath came into them the
slain lived and stood upon their feet, an exceedingly great
host.

This vision has no immediate reference to what we now
call 'the resurrection of the dead'. Ezekiel gives his own
authoritative interpretation of what the vision means. The
bones stand for the whole house of Israel. Israel had been
exiled to a land of death in Babylon. Babylon was very
much like Sheol. There Israel was shorn of her glory; she
lost continuity with her past, and her traditional temple
worship. 'By the waters of Babylon, there we sat down and
wept, when we remembered Zion . . . How shall we sing
the Lord's song in a foreign land?' (Ps. 137:1, 4)

Ezekiel promises that God will redeem his people from
their hell. Israel's bones have been dried up; hope has
vanished; the people are cut off from their roots. But God
will roll away the stone from the sepulchre of exile: 'Thus
says the Lord God: Behold, I will open your graves. . . O
my people. . . and I will put my Spirit within you, and you
shall live, and I will place you in your own land' (Ezek. 37:
12–14).

If exile is a state of death, return from exile is a resurrection. The image plainly refers to the happiness which the
whole people will experience at the recovery of their land
and heritage.

Time passed and Israel, through the doubts of wise men
like Qoheleth, came to a belief in life after death. Death is
too arbitrary an event to shatter the relationship between
God and his people. God's fidelity to his covenant demands

a life beyond the grave. But how could they depict this except in the resurrection terms of Ezekiel? Already in the second century BC, Daniel has a tremendous, bewildering vision of the messianic times which will come after 'a time of trouble'. 'And many of those who sleep in the dust of the earth shall awake, some to everlasting life, and some to shame and everlasting contempt' (12:2). The Pharisees in particular championed the resurrection of the dead: at the consummation of all things, the dead will all rise together and stand up in joy before the Lord.

In New Testament times, the Sadducees were still opposing this belief on strongly traditionalist grounds. There is no mention of it, they claimed, in the first five books of Moses, the Torah. The Sadducees did not prevail.

CHRIST THE RESURRECTION AND THE LIFE

Jesus accepted the untraditional Pharisaic belief and in the precise terms in which he learned it: the resurrection of the body. Jesus never questioned the fact that God who alone was good was the God of Abraham, Isaac and Jacob, the God of the living not the dead. In John's gospel, Jesus promises that all who share his life by communing with his body and blood will also share in his resurrection: 'He who eats my flesh and drinks my blood has eternal life, and I will raise him up at the last day' (6:54). He tells Martha, whose brother Lazarus has died: 'I am the resurrection and the life; he who believes in me, though he die, yet shall he live, and whoever lives and believes in me shall never die' (11:25).

When, at Pentecost, the disciples came to talk about Jesus' triumph over the scandalous cross, they instinctively spoke in Pharisaic terms of Jesus being raised from the dead. His cause had seemed lost; he descended without hope into Sheol, the kingdom of the dead. But he rose again 'in a little while', on the third day which we call Easter Sunday.

In Jesus' case, the disciples believed, God forestalled the general resurrection at the end of time. Time is turned back on itself so that the Glory to come is made present in the risen Christ. He is the first born from the dead, the first fruits of them that sleep.

But John's gospel anticipates Easter day itself by taking up once more an image from the Book of Genesis and transforming it. 'When Jesus had received the vinegar, he said, "It is finished"; and he bowed his head and gave up his spirit' (19:30). In Mark, Jesus spoke in Ezekiel's terms of the Son of Man coming on the clouds of heaven at the end of days to 'gather his elect from the four winds, from the ends of the earth to the ends of heaven' (13:27). But in John, Jesus' dying breath is already the Breath of God by which mankind lives; his expiration is our in-Spiration. At the very moment when Jesus dies, the Spirit of resurrection is let loose and blows like the breath of Spring across the world. This is the Spirit which Jesus breathed on his disciples on Easter day as the Forgiveness of Sins. This is the Spirit whose breath reached gale force on the day of Pentecost. The same Spirit will breathe on the dry bones of the world at the last day when the whole face of the earth is to be renewed (Ps. 104:30).

At his resurrection Jesus is the Lord of creation (Gen. 1:26) and this is why it is he who now says: 'You shall know that I am the Lord when I open your graves, and raise you from your graves, O my people. And I will put my Spirit within you, and you shall live, and I will place you in your own land.'

By his Spirit, Christ will raise up all of us together 'at the last day'. Why the stress on the last day? Because humanity is a single man, Adam. The body is 'common clay'; it binds us each to each. The body binds Jesus to us and us to him for ever.

Another way of putting it is to say that mankind, of which Jesus is the head, forms a single family so that even Christ cannot be counted fully blessed until all the family are reunited. The happiness of everyone deepens and extends the happiness of everyone else. This is precisely why the Hebrews never took to the idea of the immortality of the soul. The individual soul sounds so naked, so alone. They preferred to follow Ezekiel in speaking of the resurrection of the body; this emphasizes that we are whole and entire human beings and that each person is parcelled up in every other person. Above all, 'the resurrection of the body' makes it clear that we do not survive death by means of some intrinsically incorrupt element in our nature, namely, soul. We do *not* survive death; we conquer it. And we conquer it by the power of the Spirit of God who comes upon us and raises us to the new life God is eager to bestow on his children in Jesus Christ.

But we still walk in the valley of the shadow of death. 'The last enemy to be destroyed,' wrote Paul, 'is death' (1 Cor. 15:26). Death is of man's creation as W. B. Yeats expressed so vividly:

> Nor dread nor hope attend
> A dying animal;
> A man awaits his end
> Dreading and hoping all;
> Many times he died
> Many times rose again.
> A great man in his pride
> Confronting murderous men
> Casts derision upon
> Supersession of breath;
> He knows death to the bone –
> Man has created death.[25]

Yes, man has created death but he cannot kill it. However much death is derided, it washes all before it like the sea. Even the brave man Christ sweated blood at the prospect on the following day of 'supersession of breath'. It did not matter that he was afraid and Socrates was not. He was dying the death of all men. And he trusted in a much greater Breath than that which animated his mortal frame.

It does not matter very much in our case either if we are afraid of death. To tell the truth, some of us are and some are not. This does not seem to me to have a great deal to do with faith. Fools can die bravely and wise men with trembling and tears. Like Christ we may have to offer God not only our death but our fear of death as well. Perhaps there is a special form of bravery by which men are not afraid to be afraid of this last enemy, death.

Fearless or afraid, those who have been 'Christened' by faith, hope and love belong to Christ and eagerly await his coming when he will 'change our lowly body to be like his glorious body, by the power which enables him even to subject all things to himself' (Phil. 3:20–21). The 'power' is the Spirit, the Breath of God.

All mankind began to live when God first breathed into Adam's nostrils; all mankind began to live again when Christ breathed his last Breath over the face of the earth. This is the Breath that cannot die; man will not return for ever to the dust. 'The world,' Pope John said, 'wasn't built to be a cemetery.' 'If the Breath of him who raised Jesus from the dead dwells in you, he who raised Christ Jesus from the dead will give life to your mortal bodies also through his Breath which dwells in you' (Rom. 8:11).

THINGS UNSEEN AND ETERNAL

Throughout the ages men have disagreed about what happens after death. Some have doubted whether anything 'happens'. In a brilliant if empty argument, Epicurus said:

'Do not be afraid of death for that is to be afraid of something you will never meet. While you are here, death is not. And when death is here, you are not.' Few people have been consoled by such an approach; they suspect that when death comes, they will 'still be around somehow somewhere'.

It is, in fact, hard to imagine the complete cessation of oneself. Sartre acknowledged this in his short story, 'The Wall'. The time: the Spanish Civil War. The place: a Falangist gaol. Tom, a member of the International Brigade, is awaiting execution. He says to Pablo, a fellow prisoner:

> It's like a nightmare . . . I tell myself there will be nothing afterwards. But I don't understand what it means. Sometimes I almost can . . . and then it fades away and I start thinking about the pains again, bullets, explosions. I'm a materialist, I swear it to you; I'm not going crazy. But something's the matter. I see my corpse; that's not hard but *I'm* the one who sees it, with *my* eyes. I've got to think . . . think that I won't see anything anymore and the world will go on for the others. We aren't made to think that, Pablo.[26]

In *Doctor Zhivago*, Anna Ivanovna Gromekó, suffering from severe pleurisy, has the same experience: 'Death is hanging over me . . . Any moment . . . When you go to have a tooth out you're frightened, it'll hurt, you prepare yourself . . . But this isn't a tooth . . . it's the whole of you, your whole life . . . being pulled out . . . And what does it mean? Nobody knows . . .'[27]

Even those who have repudiated the Christian image of resurrection – thinking, mistakenly, that it entails the revivifying of a corpse – have generally hesitated before dismissing altogether the notion of post-mortem survival. For example, John Stuart Mill, the great nineteenth-century free-thinker, demurred – with a touching inconsistency –

at the intolerable prospect of never again seeing his dead wife, Harriet. It is not easy to accept the final extinction of loved ones in whom one has sensed something unseen and eternal.

Socrates was perhaps the wisest of Athenians. When he was about to die – though he conceded that he did not know what awaited him in the grave – he made this splendid if limited confession of faith: 'This one thing you must take as true: no evil can happen to a good man living or dead.' Perhaps Socrates' confession is not so limited, after all; for in it he expresses complete confidence in the *moral* character of the universe. It is this sense of the moral character underlying all experience that has encouraged people to believe or at least hope that death will not separate loving human beings from each other. Even in the case of those thinkers – many of whom are the noblest mankind has produced – who have explicitly denied life after death, we can take consolation in this thought: far more important than belief in life after death is fidelity to life itself. But is it possible, someone may ask, to be upright and holy without any conviction that there is life after death? What more can I do than give a short list of some men who fall into that category: Abraham, Isaac, Jacob, Moses, Aaron, Joshua, David, Solomon, Hezechiah, Josiah, Isaiah, Jeremiah, Ezekiel. God will reward those who have loved without any thought of reward.

If Christians believe in life after death, it is because they experience daily a communion with Jesus Christ who died two thousand years ago and was raised by God to a new life in the Spirit. This communion allows them no doubts or hesitations. They *know* their 'Redeemer liveth', and with St Paul they say:

So we do not lose heart. Though our outer nature is wasting away, our inner nature is being renewed every day. For this slight momentary affliction is preparing for us an eternal weight of glory beyond all comparison, because we look not to the things that are seen but to the things that are unseen; for the things that are seen are transient, but the things that are unseen are eternal. For we know that if the earthly tent we live in is destroyed, we have a building from God, a house not made with hands, eternal in the heavens . . . He who has prepared us for this very thing is God, who has given us the Spirit as a guarantee (2 Cor. 4:16–5:1, 5).

Spirit of Jesus, Wind, Water, Fire, come!
Spirit of Jesus, God's Anointing, come!
Spirit of Jesus, our Consoler, come!
Spirit of Jesus, loving Heart of God, come!
Spirit of Jesus, Dove of divine peace, come!
Spirit of Jesus, First fruits of the Glory, come!
Spirit of Jesus, Breath of the world's Resurrection, come!

Discussion questions

Are you afraid of death or of dying or of both? Is it in some sense un-Christian to be afraid of death? What is it that makes some people fearless and some terrified in the face of death?

How did Christ approach death? What does the fourth gospel mean by the words which describe his death: 'He bowed his head and gave up his Spirit' (19:30)?

Do most of your friends believe in life after death? What arguments are put forward by those who deny it? How do you counter such arguments? Is it possible to lead a deep moral life without belief in God and life everlasting?

Is it immoral to do something simply to earn a reward in heaven?

In what sense has man created death?

Is it likely that city-dwellers are less close to God and spiritual realities than people who dwell in rural areas?

Which of the images representing the Spirit has appealed to you most? Do you feel that it is necessary to return now to a more abstract approach to 'the third person of the Trinity'?

Afterword

> Oh, my luve's like a red, red rose,
> That's newly sprung in June;
> Oh, my luve's like the melodie
> That's sweetly played in tune.[28]

In that single verse, Robert Burns manages to convey a great deal of what lovers feel about each other. The marvel is that he does so more precisely and more memorably than any number of volumes on psychology and physiology. Using only the simplest images and rhymes, he goes on to express the longing of lovers to keep faithful to each other through their lives:

> Till a' the seas gang dry, my dear,
> And the rocks melt wi' the sun:
> I will luve thee still, my dear,
> While the sands o' life shall run.

Whatever else the Jewish-Christian religion is, it is certainly *a poem*, a poem of epic dimensions. Theologians and exegetes, like psychologists and physiologists, do a sturdy and irreplaceable job. But only the artistry of the poets who wrote the Bible and their mostly anonymous successors who compiled the liturgy bears comparison with something as beautiful as 'My Love is like a Red, Red Rose'.

To find a rival to Burns's poem we would have to turn to the brilliant and moving story in Genesis in which God takes Man's rib, encloses it in flesh and builds a woman out of it. This is the first poem to be found in scripture:

> The Man exclaimed:
>> 'This at last is bone from my bones,
>> and flesh from my flesh!
>> This is to be called Wo-man,
>> for this was taken from Man.'

This is why a man leaves his father and mother and joins himself to his wife, and they become one body (Gen. 2:22–24).

Or we could choose for comparison with Burns the passage in Ephesians which orchestrates the Genesis theme. The author says:

Husbands should love their wives as their own bodies. He who loves his wife loves himself. For no man ever hates his own flesh, but nourishes and cherishes it, as Christ does the church, because we are members of his body. 'For this reason a man shall leave his father and mother and be joined to his wife, and the two shall become one flesh' (Eph. 5:28–31).

Finally, we could turn to the poetry of the Church's liturgy of marriage:

> I, John, take thee, Mary,
> to my lawful wedded wife,
> to have and to hold from this day forward,
> for better for worse, for richer for poorer,
> in sickness and in health, to love and to cherish,
> till death do us part.

Clearly, we could more easily translate Burns's poem into a scientific treatise on love than translate the Bible's poetry on the man-woman relationship into an academic treatise on theology. The same is to be said of the Bible's teaching on the relationship between God and man.

In this case, the poetry employed centres on the Holy Spirit. It communicates to us that God our Creator really loves us. More, it conveys that God cannot be the unknowing, unfeeling deity of Greek philosophy but entirely personal and loving in himself. How could we possibly *feel* his love for us unless he himself *is* Love? This is why scripture speaks not merely of God but of God's Word and God's Spirit. Through all the compressed and often confusing language of creeds and dogmas this has never altered. To be truthful to our experience of the divine Mystery we are obliged to speak of God (known in Christ to be Father), his Word (present in the whole world and made flesh in Jesus Christ) and the Spirit (the Breath of life omnipresent but let loose with a new violence in the world with the first Pentecostal preaching of Christ's death and resurrection). Bible and liturgy are not simply more beautiful but in a sense more *true* than abstract, credal formulas. Like Burns's poem about human love, they convey immediately and lucidly what we feel is true about God. This is particularly so in the case of the Spirit who has been the subject of this book.

The liturgy is marvellous at Advent: think of the yearning tone of the *Rorate Coeli*. At Christmas: the carols make even atheists wish they were believers. At the Easter Vigil: there is the soaring, evocative song of the Exultet around the Easter candle which represents the risen Christ. But at Pentecost the Church seems to have excelled herself.

I recall as a college student going into chapel on Whitsuntide evenings and joining in what I still feel to be the Church's finest hymns, *Veni Creator Spiritus* (with which all solemn councils of the Church begin) and *Veni Sancte Spiritus* which for me is unsurpassable. Always it was summer; a warm June evening; roses everywhere, the colour of Pentecostal flame; the simple plain-chant melodies.

It seemed a good idea to end this book with these two great songs to the Holy Spirit in a new translation. They are proof that even in the academic atmosphere of medieval times, the Christian community never lost touch in its prayers with its biblical heritage or with the elemental images of water and wind, light and fire.

Veni Sancte Spiritus

Holy Spirit, come, we pray,
And a single heavenly ray
   Of thy Light to us impart.

Come thou Father of the poor,
Come thou Gift which will endure,
   Come thou Brightness of the heart.

Of Consolers thou art best,
In our hearts the dearest Guest,
   Dearest Friend through all the years.

After work our Rest at night,
Shade against the sun's fierce light,
   Solace when we are in tears.

Of all lights thou loveliest Light,
Shine on us and chase the night
   From the crannies of our soul.

Nothing is more certain than
Without thee there is in man
   Nothing innocent or whole.

Cleanse us of each sinful stain,
Soak our dryness with thy rain,
   Soothe and heal what suffers pain.

Unbend fast the bigot's brain,
Fan all fires that start to wane,
   Bring the lost sheep home again.

Grant thy seven-fold Gift to those
In whose heart thy mercy flows,
   Those with faith and trust in thee.

Grant them virtue's rich reward,
Grant them death in Christ their Lord,
   Grant them joy eternally.

Veni Creator Spiritus

Come, thou Creator-Spirit, come,
Be thou our spirit's fondest Guest,
Thy grace send down on us, and blest
Shall be the heart within our breast.

Thou who art called the Comforter,
God's Gift exceeding our desire,
The living Spring, the Love, the Fire,
God's Oil to comfort and inspire.

Thou art the Father's seven-fold Gift,
Finger of God with which he makes
New worlds of beauty for our sakes
And gives the Breath of Life – and takes.

Be thou the Light within our head,
Within our hearts be thou the Flame,
Be thou the Strength, always the same,
That courses through our feeble frame.

Far from us make the Tempter fly,
Grant now thy peace for which we long.
With thee as Guide we will be strong
And wise enough to shun all wrong.

Through thee, O Spirit, may we know
The Eternal Father and the Son,
Believing, till life's course is run,
Thou art the Love that makes them one.

References

1. *Three Tales*, Signet, New York, 1964.
2. *Gerard Manley Hopkins*, Penguin, London, 1953, p. 27.
3. Bodley Head, London, 1937, pp. 316–17.
4. *Waiting On God*, Routledge and Kegan Paul, London, 1951, p. 27, and Fontana, London, 1959, p. 42.
5. *Poems Of Robert Browning*, Oxford University Press, London 1959, 'Bishop Blougram's Apology', p. 428.
6. *Peter Abelard*, Panther, London, p. 167.
7. T. S. Eliot, *Collected Poems 1909–1962*, Faber, London, 1963, p. 212.
8. Hodder and Stoughton, London, 1974.
9. Dietrich Bonhoeffer, *Letters And Papers From Prison*, Fontana, London, 1959, p. 56.
10. *Ibid.* p. 61.
11. Laurens van der Post, *The Heart Of The Hunter*, Penguin, London, 1965, p. 204.
12. T. E. Lawrence, *The Seven Pillars Of Wisdom*, Jonathan Cape, London, 1940, p. 38.
13. C. S. Lewis, *The Four Loves*, Fontana, London, 1963, pp. 119–20.
14. Alexander Solzhenitsyn, *The First Circle*, Fontana, London, 1970, p. 142.
15. See *Soledad Brother, The Prison Letters Of George Jackson*, Penguin, London, 1971 – a brilliant and moving book.
16. Junichiro Tanizaki, *Seven Japanese Tales*, Berkley Publishing Corp., 1965.
17. Mentor Books, New York, 1960, p. 23.
18. *Léon Bloy, Pilgrim Of The Absolute*, ed. Raissa Maritain, Eyre and Spottiswoode, London, 1947, p. 349.
19. In 'Angel Levine', *The Magic Barrel*, Penguin, London, 1968, p. 48.

20. *Op. cit.*, p. 283.
21. *The Snow Queen And Other Tales*, Signet, New York, 1966.
22. Isaac Babel, *Collected Stories*, Penguin, London, 1961, p. 220.
23. Leo Tolstoy, *Anna Karenin*, tr. Rosemary Edmonds, Penguin, London, 1969, p. 733.
24. From an unpublished verse rendering of the Book of Ecclesiastes.
25. 'Death' in *Collected Poems Of W. B. Yeats*, Macmillan, London, 1971, p. 264.
26. Jean-Paul Sartre, *Intimacy*, Panther, London, 1960, p. 60.
27. Boris Pasternak, *Doctor Zhivago*, Fontana, London, 1961, p. 80.
28. The Poetical Works Of Robert Burns, Chandos Classics, London and New York, p. 433.

What is Real in Christianity?
DAVID L. EDWARDS

The author strips away the legends from Jesus to show the man who is real, relevant and still fascinating. A clear, confident statement of Christian faith taking account of all criticisms.

The First Christmas
H. J. RICHARDS

Can one really believe in the seventies in such improbable events as the Virgin Birth, the shepherds and the angels, the Magi and the star in the East? Are they just fables? This book suggests that they might be the wrong questions to ask, and may even prevent the reader from arriving at the deeper issues. What these deeper issues are is here explained with clarity, simplicity and honesty.

Wrestling with Christ
LUIGI SANTUCCI

'This is a most unusual book, a prolonged meditation of the life of Christ using many changing literary forms, dialogue, description, addresses to Christ, passages of self-communing. It is written by a Christian passionately concerned that everyone should know Jesus Christ.' *Catholic Herald*

Journey for a Soul
GEORGE APPLETON

'Wherever you turn in this inexpensive but extraordinarily valuable paperback you will benefit from sharing this man's pilgrimage of the soul.'
Methodist Recorder

Also available in the Fontana Religious Series

The Boundaries of Our Being
PAUL TILLICH

Paul Tillich is generally regarded as the greatest English-speaking theologian of the twentieth century. In this volume are collected his magnificent series of sermons preached in universities and colleges between 1947 and 1963 and previously published as two books, *The New Being* and *The Eternal Now*.

The Courage To Be
PAUL TILLICH

The problem of anxiety has dominated much of contemporary literature and philosophy. In this book Paul Tillich tries to point the way toward its conquest.

Apologia Pro Vita Sua
J. H. NEWMAN

A passionate defence of Cardinal Newman's own intellectual and spiritual integrity by a man who had been under continuous attack for many years.

Newman's Journey
MERIOL TREVOR

'An exemplary life of Newman. Miss Trevor writes exceedingly well and turns the most arid of controversy to stimulus. Miss Trevor has splendidly put together the facts.'

Observer